LEWIS MUMFORD:
A BIBLIOGRAPHY

LEWIS MUMFORD:
A BIBLIOGRAPHY
1914–1970

ELMER S. NEWMAN

With an Introduction by
LEWIS MUMFORD

Harcourt Brace Jovanovich, Inc., New York

First edition
ISBN 0-15-154750-5
Library of Congress Catalog Card Number: 72-160407
Printed in the United States of America
A B C D E

To those who will widen the trails
Lewis Mumford has blazed

PREFACE

My AIM in compiling this bibliography has been to organize and present a complete record of the work of Lewis Mumford in all its published forms, *e.g.*, books and pamphlets, letters to the editor, book reviews. A few incidental items have been omitted. I have selected a number of categories, according to the various forms of his work, and listed each citation in its appropriate place. As the work of writers as wide-ranging as Mumford does not always fit into neat classifications, I have added prefatory notes to some categories to explain their scope. The arrangement in each category is chronological; this seemed a natural form to follow as it suggests the direction of Mumford's thought and the concentration of his interest.

Many of Mumford's articles and other writings, particularly after 1945, have been reprinted in periodicals and books. I have not attempted to cite every publication where such reprints have appeared. But, in some instances, I have listed periodicals and books where reprints have been published. I did this when I felt an additional listing would make an article or other work more readily available, as in the case where it originally appeared in a publication of limited circulation or availability. I have tried to cite, in all instances, the publication where each work originally appeared. Where an article or other work, originally published in a periodical or book, was later included in a collection of Mumford's essays and other writings, I have added a note to the citation giving the title of the collection where the work can be found.

Although it was not my purpose to compile an annotated bibliography, I have added explanatory notes to a number of entries. I did this in order to give a fuller identification to an item where I felt this was needed.

I hope that this bibliography will assist and encourage specialists and generalists alike to look more closely at the work of Lewis Mumford and to evaluate his more than half a century of creative effort.

November 1970   ESN

ACKNOWLEDGMENTS

I owe a profound debt of gratitude to Lewis Mumford for the encouragement he gave me and for the many kindnesses he extended to me during the period this bibliography was in preparation. He helped me clarify numerous obscure details, gave me full access to his personal files, and reviewed my manuscript at two different points in its preparation. His willing assistance and sound counsel spared me many hours of search time and much lengthy correspondence. I wish also to give special thanks to Mrs. Mumford for her warm hospitality during my two visits to the Mumford home in Amenia, New York. This association with the Mumfords was a wonderful and unexpected joy that developed out of the preparation of this bibliography.

I am also indebted to my colleague Carrol Gensert, inter-library loan librarian at Sears Library of Case Western Reserve University, who spared no effort in helping me locate many periodicals and other publications not available in the Cleveland area.

CONTENTS

INTRODUCTION

VIEWED ABSTRACTLY, a bibliography is as devoid of human interest as a time table or a telephone directory—except for those who have a practical need to verify a date or find an article. Superficially, what the reader will find here is but the barest outline of my writings over something more than half a century; just sufficient to guide him to a bookseller or a library. With reason he will say with Charles Lamb that this is one of those books that is no book at all: merely a series of printed pages between covers. I myself shared that feeling when Mr. Newman first approached me with the proposal to compile such a bibliography. In the nature of things this could be only a labor of love, and I marveled that my writings could evoke so much love, when the task itself seemed so glaringly sterile, so utterly unrewarding.

But how wrong I was! In reacting this way I was curiously overlooking my own experience. For though my purpose has not been that of a librarian or a bibliographer, the fact is that since 1933 I myself have compiled a formidable series of bibliographies, none of them less than 372 items, one almost a thousand, to serve as background to my extensive surveys: the most recent bibliography, that in *The Pentagon of Power*, contains 475 items. Though such bibliographies are but the first stage in reading and evaluating books, there are moments when the compilation of a preliminary bibliography induces an anticipatory interest, which every new book that proves rewarding intensifies; and at the end of one's work, when one is finally putting together the entire list, and checking it for accuracy in titles and dates, the list of books itself results in a simmer of excitement, like that produced by any minor work of art. In some cases, this pleasure is intensified by the environment: the hours I have spent in the catalog room of the New York Public Library on Fifth Avenue searching out new titles, or checking up on those used, I would put among the rewarding moments of my life: all the more because, before great libraries began to suffer from the mass production of books and periodicals and the consequent congestion of catalog space, that hall, in its lofty amplitude, elevated one's mind and eased one's work. In those days the catalog room induced a benign feeling akin to Henry James's "Great Good Place," "all beautified by omissions."

As for that catalog itself, I count it not merely as the best organized I have used anywhere, a royal bibliography of bibliographies, but as one of the wonders of the human mind—no less wonderful than the computer, though all the materials of which it is composed, the wood, the paper, the print, the human brains, antedate—and will possibly outlast—the electronic and microchemical media that threaten to supplant it. That the Central Library's alphabetic three-letter system of identifying the books, invented by Dr. John Shaw Billings, has not been imitated everywhere—indeed has been "obliterated" by the deceptively simple Dewey system, or by even more cumbrous variations—is a silent reproach against the guild of librarians. But I must not ride this particular hobby horse further: my purpose is only to do justice to the greatness of New York's Central Library, neglected though it has been by the municipality.

Though I readily accept the drudgery involved in verifying a long bibliography—and only once relinquished it to another hand—my personal bibliographies have one quality that would be inappropriate for such an austere and extensive catalog as Mr. Newman has compiled: they are spiced with my personal comments, occasionally scarifying or—even worse!—mischievous, on some of the works I have been condemned to read. There have been moments, in looking over Mr. Newman's compilation, when I have wondered if it would not be amusing, and even profitable, to interlard it with comments of my own. There are sundry good reasons for resisting this temptation. But perhaps the best reason is that I possess an alter ego who is severer than any other critic of my works, and who on occasion has a malicious pleasure in taking me down—and incidentally, alas! taking the reader in—by making disparaging remarks about my actual achievements, and diminishing their claims to attention.

This is a private joke between the author and his alter ego: but unfortunately too many academic minds have taken over the alter ego's modest estimates, and to be safe have reduced them even further. In order to avoid the very serious risk of being unjust to my own work, I have prudently decided to forgo any critical commentary.

But there are other matters that warrant the making of this bibliography. Though Mr. Newman, as a trained university librarian, has all the resources of the whole American library system at his command, and has made full use of them, it still was not possible for him to make an exhaustive compilation without utilizing data that only I possessed, since some of those data escaped the standard catalogs and existed only in my files of published work, or on my own library shelves. So, after considerable preliminary correspondence, he visited me in my home in the country and spent the greater part of a week, but for nights at our local inn, under my roof. Happily he was not always immured in the filing room. We had many occasions for consultation throughout the day, and from time to time would stretch our legs by a walk around the home acres, so we got to know each other, to our mutual advantage, as human beings; and this daily intimacy increased our confidence in each other. While I marveled over how much Mr. Newman had been able to get hold of unaided, he unburied items that even I had forgotten. And incidentally, he discovered from my files a puzzling fact he has told me of about the early variant editions of the same issues of *The New Yorker*, local and out of town. This discovery will put other librarians on guard against taking for granted that their early files of *The New Yorker* necessarily cover all its articles.

This human relation between us would not have been surprising in an older day, when frequent exchanges by both letter and face-to-face meetings took place. But in an age overexcited by the convenience of the telephone and the magic of computers, this demonstration of the value of personal communication is worth mentioning: no computer, however programmed, could have discovered what this human bibliographer dis-covered. When the current United States Catalog of Books was set up by a computer, a large swathe of essential items—the contents of two whole letters of the alphabet—had dropped out before anyone discovered this gross omission in the printed work itself; and similar lapses might easily have occurred with this bibliography but for the fact that Mr. Newman and I are both, happily, members of the human race, and are capable of discovering and correcting our own errors of omission and commission—while nevertheless acknowledging that, despite all our efforts, we may still have passed over significant items that somehow remained out of sight or out of mind. The fact that Mr. Newman and I have con-fidence in each other is something that should give a degree of confidence to those who make use of this compilation.

So far, I have been dealing only with the preparatory work on the bibliography. But it has had other human results, too. At the time the search came to a head, I had just finished *The Pentagon of Power*, and was beginning to play with the notion, once I had taken a rest, of resum-ing work on an autobiography, which I had begun as far back as 1956. At this juncture, it suddenly became plain to me that Mr. Newman had unwittingly made a grand gift to my autobiography: he had shown me, in however severe outline, the totality of my life's work, in so far as that work had an independent existence in print. This was, so to say, a shadow biography; and when I beheld it in all its richness—a thousand items or so, Mr. Newman tells me—I experienced such a shock as one gets when one hears one's voice played back by a recorder for the first time.

Though most of the concrete evidence of my written work exists on my bookshelves and in my filing cases, it is only in the condensed form of a bibliography that one can take in this immense collection at a glance. If anyone should ask me what I have been doing with my life, I could point to the bibliography and say: This. At least "this" is a shorthand summary of a major part of that life; and when one begins to interpret this evidence, it moves one to self-examination.

At first glance, the very size of this catalog is appalling. Does this mean that I, who have been a foe of mere quantification all my life, have betrayed my sociological insights and my ethical standards? Fortunately for my peace of mind, the evidence is more favorable than a casual reader might think. Since my major vocation is that of a writer, a certain level of productivity would seem a major economic condition for remaining alive. But, forgetting books and duplicate items, a thousand items over fifty years brings an average of twenty articles a year; or, roughly, one every two and a half weeks. Not a few of these items are under a thousand words each. Compared to people who sought bigger incomes, or were trapped in their choice of media and forced to produce many times this amount of copy, I may boast that I have not seriously contributed to either environmental pollution or mental depletion.

But what about *books?* The total count of all my books is only twenty-four. Compared with popular writers, with a genius for catching the public eye and suiting the public palate, this number is trivial: many novelists, including intellectually reputable ones like Anthony Trollope or H. G. Wells, turn out sixty or eighty books in the course of a lifetime. But long ago I decided that, no matter what the financial exigencies might be, I must limit my output of books, if I hoped to be read by a later generation. What I mean here by a book is strictly a work planned in advance to be a whole, not a mere collection of essays, whether mixed or on a single topic; and though I have indeed put out such books, I have sought wherever possible to do so in an ephemeral physical form, that is, as paperbacks. Yet the paperback edition of *Men Must Act*, in 1939, which came out well before paperbacks had begun to make a mass market of their own, ironically sold fewer copies than the hard-cover edition.

Putting aside such collections, I have, in forty-eight years, produced only seventeen books. There are of course many scholars, like Gibbon, who have made a notable reputation on a bare half-dozen books or less: but they had other sources of income. For one who is a writer by vocation —who is mainly dependent upon his writing for support—seventeen would seem to be close to the minimum. And I have been rewarded for this abstemiousness: my first seven books are still in print, and my first book, *The Story of Utopias*, has virtually never been out of print through half a century—though it surely doesn't deserve such pre-eminence. None of my major books, furthermore, for the last twenty-five years has been dropped by the publisher, except *Green Memories*. So there would seem to be a case for continence, if not for total abstinence, in order to hold down the excessive birth rate of books.

Looked at from this angle, this bibliography brings me a certain reassurance. But what must I say about the vast miscellaneous assortment of articles, essays, reviews, introductions that contributed a necessary portion of my income—though never enough to enable me to forgo occasional lectures, visiting professorships, and even for two limited periods, a regular lectureship and a regular professorial appointment. When I look at the contents of these reviews, I can see how from the very beginning they were often early jottings and notes for the books that I was eventually to write. Always, my personal and intellectual interests took precedence over economic necessities, even in lean periods. Though certain dominant themes begin, before the thirties, to emerge from the vast welter of reflections and reactions, the most useful part played by these seemingly indiscriminate sallies is that they invaded, if only for a short look-around, many widely separated territories: expeditions from which I brought home fruits, like the scouts who went ahead in Canaan, which I would preserve and draw on only at a much later period. Thus certain ideas expressed in an appreciative but critical review of J. S. Haldane's *Mechanism, Life, and Personality* (1921), pervade, in fully assimilated state, my presentation of the organic world picture in *The Pentagon of Power*.

If I had cast my life in the role of a certified specialist, this miscellaneous searching and writing would have been suicidal: no university would receive, much less advance, a man who, even if he wrote much, was so indiscriminate in his appetites, so wanton in his invasion of distant fields that he had no academic license to cultivate. When, therefore, the offer to teach came first in 1930 from Dartmouth College, I embarked on my work there as a full professor, without any chagrin over my academic nudity. Happily, in so far as I have any reputation as a scholar, it is not as a specialist but as a generalist; and only by ranging as widely as I did as a writer could I have prepared myself for that special task. As a writer I had a freedom no young Ph.D. could hope for till he was too old to profit by it. At what university, I ask myself now, could I have had a similar freedom, a similar stimulus, or a similar opportunity to break loose from prevailing academic patterns?

My one concern about this lengthy catalog of my writings is over its possible misuse: might it not tempt some academic candidate, seeking a fresh field to explore, to give too much attention to my more ephemeral writings, and give them an undue prominence, if only because he or she alone would have for the nonce the distinction of being the first to analyze them? The real advantage of such an exhaustive list, rather, is that it should make it easier to get hold of and quickly dismiss my more hasty or otherwise negligible articles and papers. As background material, they will do little harm, and even, in the hands of a serious student, perhaps do a little good. But there is a risk that they may be pushed into the foreground, and even treated as if they were superior to my mature works, much as Van Wyck Brooks's more callow early essays have recently been rated as his central contribution, to the utter disparagement of his Makers and Finders series. I have been put on guard against this happening by the pair of urban sociologists who chose my earliest essay on "The City" (1922) for publication in a book of readings, and have in their critical comment misrepresented the whole tendency of my work on cities, which they are, seemingly, ignorant of.

But there is still another side to a comprehensive bibliography which the author should perhaps dwell on a moment. It has called my attention, as never before, to the fact that such a list, even while it shows the extent of my literary and scholarly commitments, in so far as they found publication, still exhibits only a part of my life as writer: the commissions need to be qualified by the omissions; for those omissions are, so to say, the dark, unexposed side of the moon. What a writer has written and *not* published is in some ways even more revealing than what he has finally thought fit to expose. Many of the manuscripts that I have preserved through some squirrel-like hoarding impulse never merited publication, or to be more honest, they should have been destroyed almost at once. Yet somehow they give a certain substance and definition to what has gone into print. I say nothing about my "juvenilia": we were all young once, and even some of my published writings—I won't single them out! —deserve to be classed as juvenilia.

Among my unpublished writings, however, are four whole books and one half-finished work I never submitted to a publisher. Add to this the unfinished manuscript of an early novel, a May basket of poems, a series of one-act plays, and two finished full-length plays, the latest dated 1928, and so vast in its scope that it could only be handled as a motion picture. (The theme of the latter, incidentally, centered around the Brooklyn Bridge and two quite imaginary Roeblings, the younger bearing a suspicious resemblance to myself, whose lives were intertwined with the New York of their day and the building of the bridge. As it happened, I conceived this theme while living on Brooklyn Heights, where Hart Crane, who was then occupying an apartment in Roebling's very house, was writing *his* poem, "The Bridge.") Whatever else these rejections and repressions may mean, they at least show that I have practiced what I preached: selectivity, not unbridled production.

As for the books, one of them was a series of six lectures on American architecture, given at Harvard University in the autumn of 1939. They never satisfied me, since I had not been able to spare the time for fresh exploration and research. The second was an unpublished novel in free verse, two published excerpts of which are included in the bibliography. This was a highly promising work; but the war interrupted it and I could never recapture the inner turmoil that was essential for a final rewriting of it. The fourth was a series of observations, in the manner of La Rochefoucauld, on Love and Marriage.

But the most formidable unpublished manuscript is the most teasing of all, for its immediate failure was offset by an unforeseen success. After the one-volume condensation of A. J. Toynbee's *A Study of History* had come out, I conceived that it might be equally helpful if some patient sympathetic scholar would produce a one-volume version of The Renewal of Life series. But junior generalists, unlike junior historians, are hard to find: certainly none came forward. So I decided that I myself would produce the equivalent, not by piecing together the parts of the four books, but by recasting their material around a dominant theme: that of the human personality, in all its ideal projections and actual realizations. In arriving at this mode of synthesis, I was influenced by the work of W. H. Sheldon and by the Chicago philosophers George Mead and Charles Morris. In the course of the winter of 1954–1955 I swiftly wrote some three or four hundred pages. When, after a brief pause, I read what I had written, I realized that what I had attempted was, despite a number of fresh insights, impossible: so I thrust the manuscript aside, and never read it through again—though I suppose I may have glanced at it impatiently before I turned it over to the Van Pelt Library of the University of Pennsylvania.

But meanwhile my unconscious had been at work. That spring, responding to an invitation to write a book on religion for the World Perspectives series, I sat down and found myself writing a much more extensive treatise, which turned out to be a panorama of human history, embracing the development of both community and personality, and pointing to the future. That work, called *The Transformations of Man*, was a far better summation of my essential thought than any one-volume digest of The Renewal of Life series could have been; and what is more, it started me off on the new line that led to *The City in History* and *The Myth of the Machine*. I count myself lucky in having had the critical nerve to virtually make manure of a whole winter's work in order to let *The Transformations of Man* arise from that rich compost.

I pass over many lesser manuscripts, to say nothing of sundry letters to the editors of the New York *Times* that were never published. But there remains one considerable opus, possibly as great in volume as all my books, namely, the letters written to my friends. One part of this collection has in fact been printed: *The Van Wyck Brooks–Lewis Mumford Letters*, and another quite different set, my correspondence with Sir Frederic Osborn, is scheduled for publication in England in 1971. In addition, Mr. Newman has called attention to a few other collections that have found a home in libraries. I cannot possibly estimate how many correspondents have kept even samples of my letters, though a considerable number saved by friends now dead have come back to me. But happily for me, two of the most interesting collections have been deposited in the National Library of Scotland at Edinburgh: my letters to Patrick Geddes and Victor Branford between 1920 and 1932.

In a sense, these letters are part of the large invisible undermass of my life: what rises above ground discloses only a portion of my activity as a writer. When the social challenges I have responded to, when the intellectual issues I have raised, when the diagnoses I have made of our civilization have been superseded by other situations and other, more adequate responses, my collected letters may still have value as a human testimonial of our times, and as an uncensored sidelight upon personal relationships, at a certain moment, in a certain setting. Yet even here some of the most revealing letters will for long remain unpublishable because they concern living people and inviolable intimacies.

There is still one more sunken island not accounted for in this bibliographic chart: that is my lectures. Apart from those published, and apart from those that disappeared with the breath of the speaker—among them some of my very best performances—there is a considerable body of lectures in manuscript, either because no editor cared to print them, or because I myself had no wish to see them in print. Herewith I pronounce anathema on anyone who might be tempted, under the meretricious scholarly banner of total publication, to bring out these lectures when I and my executors are no longer at hand to prevent them. Though I don't promise not to destroy many of these myself, those that escape this funeral pyre will probably be entrusted, along with my other papers, to the University of Pennsylvania.

And then, finally, there is a more intimate batch of papers that obtruded themselves on me in the very act of going through my published work. These come under the heads of "Random Notes" and "Personalia," the earliest of which go back to my high-school years, when I used to set down pitiful little epigrams—I dared to call them that—or juvenile witticisms in a little address book; and from 1915 on, more or less inspired by Samuel Butler, I would make longer notes which might, under one of Butler's headings, have been appropriately called "Higgledy-piggledy." But I never kept a diary, and unlike Emerson or my friend Brooks, I never made a list of the books I read: so occasionally, in going through these notes, I am astonished to find myself quoting books I have no memory whatever of studying, or, even more astonishingly, making fresh observations on matters I imagined to have only recently discovered.

A good part of these notes, before 1940, were written on the cheapest grade of Manila paper: indeed, my earlier manuscripts were not merely typed on such paper but went to the printer in that form. If anyone doubts this, let him look at the manuscript of *The Golden Day*, deposited by my first Harcourt Brace editor, Charles A. Pearce ("Cap") in the Dartmouth Library, after he had bought it at an auction sale in behalf of some putatively good cause for, as I remember it, thirty dollars. Since I may never have another chance to acknowledge the debt I owe Cap for the kind of intellectual sympathy and stimulating appreciation that, even when I was a young man, he gave me, let me put it on record now. Being older than he, I assumed an avuncular role, more or less like Settembrini with Hans Castorp in *The Magic Mountain:* and it was part of our humor that I used to address him as "Engineer." His tastes were so catholic that in the period when he was poetry editor of *The New Yorker* they even charitably extended to my verse; and it was through him that one of my most original poems, "Fantasia on Time," saw print. I can hardly forgive the editors of the current *New Yorker Book of Poems* for leaving this poem out, though I am not sorry that they chose my six-line epigram, "Consolation in War," which Thomas Mann, I blush to mention, characterized as having the quality of an old Greek epitaph.

Mr. Newman's ferreting among my clippings brought to light first drafts of work on this same Manila paper, already darkly oxidized and crumbled at the edges, to an extent that should make them unredeemable ten years hence. Such self-effacing manuscripts could be perhaps one's most acceptable gift to posterity: for what will the world be like—indeed, what is it already?—if all our trashy thoughts are piously preserved as precious documents? This presented a genuine ethical problem: for it was not without forethought that I have rarely kept copies of my own letters, except controversial ones, which might lead to replies that in turn might call for an answer, or purely business letters, like contracts or quarrels with one's publisher, whose points needed to be kept clearly in mind until the matter was settled.

The only possible reason for keeping any of one's trivial notes is that they might be useful to a student of history or biography; and with this in mind my wife has copied them over—only to discover to her delight, in a series of notes I made before marrying her, that she was now falling in love with that vanished young man whose courtship at the time she had found, with good reason, so lacking in ardor, so unpersuasive. Those notes reveal, I must add parenthetically, that he already had a number-one wife in his literary work, and didn't quite see how he could manage to take care of a lesser mistress, too. But she was equally pleased to find that the plan of life, the discipline, the devotion to ideas that governed his later life were all there from the start.

This entire mass of notes, once committed to paper, remained practically unvisited in my later years, though at an earlier period of my life they helped me to get through more than one emotional crisis without calling upon a psychoanalyst for help. Here again, I owe another debt to Mr. Newman's patient searching. For on assaying these notes I have discovered, if not a gold mine, at least occasional veins and pockets of high-grade ore, and occasionally a real nugget. The very disparate and inconsecutive character of the notes makes them all the more interesting through their surprises; and this soon suggested a book I had never before contemplated: a Miscellany, which would hold work that had never been published—or had come out in such a limited form that it could no longer be found even in the most capacious university library.

In cataloging my books and articles, accordingly, Mr. Newman has, in effect, caused me to beget another book. Though it has not yet been assembled, I think it right to mention it here for the prospective reader, in order to make this bibliography carry my work a little forward into the future: in strict accordance with a basic principle of my philosophy, that past, present, and future must be taken in together: "for the past is still present in the future that is already here." Let us call it provisionally *A Mumford Miscellany*. In that book my future reader may even find snatches about my friendships or my loves that he will look for in vain in my autobiography—alongside, perhaps, a scene from a forgotten play, or a dialogue written in the twenties, when dialogues were anathema in almost every editorial office, except that of *The American Mercury*—though I could never find out if it was H. L. Mencken or George Jean Nathan who was bold enough to break with this traditional veto on the Dialogue. No one back in the twenties could anticipate that in another generation the tape recorder would bring into existence a new kind of dialogue, whose interminable drool, unless vigilantly edited and curtailed, will bring into existence the largest mass of mediocre non-literature that has ever been put into print. Except for a single BBC interview with Graeme Shankland—and what a brilliant performance *that* was!—I have never read the manuscript of any dialogue in which I myself took part that was worth the trouble of editing or rewriting it.

When I look at these remains of mine, or remember some of those I have already destroyed, I realize that these notes, however random, cannot be published in full; for they would give a distorted and ultimately false account of my life. My Personalia deal mostly with conflicts and crises, often at their darkest moments: unlike the sundial, they show too exclusively the clouded hours, or at the other extreme, they reveal the tenderest kind of intimacy, in personal intercourse or in sexual play, that can only be celebrated in elusive metaphor, and would shrivel under the least public exposure.

But there! In the act of contemplating this bibliography of my writings I have passed far beyond the confines of any library, and am beginning to wade knee-deep into my autobiography. Nothing could please me more about this work than the fact that Mr. Newman, by doing his job so thoroughly, has given back to me many obscure and forgotten portions of my life, and so has opened up fresh chapters that I had not heretofore contemplated even from a distance. But of course it was not for my personal use and enjoyment that he devoted himself to this work: so I trust it may prove serviceable to scholars, librarians, and even to general readers, for whom most of my writings have been invisible, or at least inaccessible beyond the passing moment. This may, in the end, take the sting out of the private family joke, between my wife Sophia and myself: that because of my indifference to the usual channels of publicity and ego-inflation, I have become, even for many scholars in my own special fields, "The Invisible Man."

LEWIS MUMFORD

Cambridge, Massachusetts
December 26, 1970

LEWIS MUMFORD:
A BIBLIOGRAPHY

A. BOOKS AND PAMPHLETS

NOTE: Only American editions are listed here, except in those instances where original publication was in England. Foreign editions are listed in a separate section.

A1 *The Story of Utopias.*
    With an introduction by Hendrik Willem Van Loon. New York: Boni and Liveright, 1922. 315p.

    Reprinted with the same title and published as follows:

    New York: Peter Smith, 1941. 315p.

    Gloucester, Mass.: Peter Smith, 1959. 315p.

    New York: Compass Book, Viking Press, 1962. 315p.
    With a new preface by Lewis Mumford; original introduction by Hendrik Willem Van Loon omitted.

A2 *Sticks and Stones; A Study of American Architecture and Civilization.*
    New York: Boni and Liveright, 1924. 247p.

    Reprinted with the same title and published as follows:

    New York: White Oak Library, W. W. Norton and Co., [1934]. 238p.
    Foreword differs slightly from that in the 1924 edition and the "Notes on Books" section contained in the earlier edition has been omitted.

    New York: Dover Publications, 1955. 238p.
    Revised edition.
    Includes a new foreword by Lewis Mumford and twenty-one plates have been added; a final paragraph has been added to each of Chapters One to Five, and to Chapter Seven; the "Notes on Books" section of the original edition has been deleted.

A3 *Aesthetics, A Dialogue.*
    Troutbeck Leaflets, No. 3. Amenia, New York: Privately printed at the Troutbeck Press, 1925. 14p.

Reprinted from the *American Mercury*, III (November 1924), 360–65, where it appeared with the title "Aesthetics: A Palaver."

A4 *The Golden Day; A Study in American Experience and Culture.*
New York: Boni and Liveright, 1926. 283p.

Reprinted with the title *The Golden Day; A Study in American Literature and Culture* and published as follows:

New York: White Oak Library, W. W. Norton and Co., [1934]. 283p.
With a new prefatory note by Lewis Mumford.

Boston: Beacon Paperback, Beacon Press, 1957. 144p.
Omits Lewis Mumford's prefatory notes contained in the 1926 and 1934 editions, but includes a new introduction by him with the title "*The Golden Day* Revisited."

New York: Dover Publications, 1968. 144p.
Includes the introduction that appeared in the 1957 edition and contains the prefatory note of the 1926 edition. A few slight corrections made in the text.

A5 *Architecture.*
Reading with a Purpose, No. 23. Chicago: American Library Association, 1926. 34p.

A6 *American Taste.*
San Francisco: The Westgate Press, 1929. 33p.

Reprinted from *Harper's Magazine*, CLV (October 1927), 569–77.

A7 *Herman Melville.*
New York: Harcourt, Brace and Co., 1929. 377p.

Also published in this edition as follows:

New York: Literary Guild of America, 1929. 377p.

Revised edition published with the title *Herman Melville, A Study of His Life and Vision.* New York: Harcourt, Brace and World, 1962. 256p.

Reprinted with the same title and published as follows:

New York: Harbinger Book, Harcourt, Brace & World, 1962, 256p.

A8 *The Brown Decades; A Study of the Arts in America, 1865–1895.*
New York: Harcourt, Brace and Co., 1931. 266p.

Reprinted with the same title and published as follows:

New York: Dover Publications, 1955. 266p.
Contains a new preface by Lewis Mumford; some slight corrections made in the text.

A9   *Technics and Civilization.*
New York: Harcourt, Brace and Co., 1934. 495p.

First volume of The Renewal of Life series.

Reprinted with the same title and published as follows:

New York: Harbinger Book, Harcourt, Brace & World, 1963. 495p.
With a new introduction by Lewis Mumford.

A10   *The Culture of Cities.*
New York: Harcourt, Brace and Co., 1938. 586p.

Second volume of The Renewal of Life series.

Reprinted with the same title and published as follows:

New York: Harvest Book, Harcourt Brace Jovanovich, 1970. 586p.
With a new preface by Lewis Mumford. This edition also re-issued in hardback in 1970.

A11   *Whither Honolulu? A Memorandum Report on Park and City Planning.*
Prepared by Lewis Mumford for City and County of Honolulu Park Board. Honolulu, T.H.: The Author, 1938. 67p.

Included in the collection of Mumford's essays, *City Development* (1945), with the title "Report on Honolulu."

A12   *Men Must Act.*
New York: Harcourt, Brace and Co., 1939. 176p.

This edition was also published in paperback in 1939 by Harcourt, Brace and Co.

A revised edition with the same title published as follows:

New York: Harcourt, Brace and Co., 1939. 176p.
With a new preface by Lewis Mumford.

The text is the same in these two editions.

A13   *Regional Planning in the Pacific Northwest: A Memorandum.*
Portland, Oregon: Northwest Regional Council, 1939. 20p.

A14   *Faith for Living.*
New York: Harcourt, Brace and Co., 1940. 333p.

This edition was published by Harcourt, Brace and Co. in 1941, as a Harbrace edition.

A15   *The South in Architecture.*
The Dancy Lectures, Alabama College, 1941.
New York: Harcourt, Brace and Co., 1941. 147p.

Reprinted with the same title and published as follows:

New York: Da Capo Press, 1967. 147p.

A16   *The School of Humanities: A Description.*
Stanford, Calif.: Stanford University, [1942]. 13p.

A17   *The Social Foundations of Post-War Building.*
Rebuilding Britain Series, No. 9. London: Faber and Faber Ltd., 1943. 40p.

Included in the collection of Mumford's essays, *City Development* (1945).

A18   *The Condition of Man.*
New York: Harcourt, Brace and Co., 1944. 467p.

Third volume in The Renewal of Life series.

A19   *The Plan of London County.*
With an editorial note by F. J. Osborn. Rebuilding Britain Series, No. 12. London: Faber and Faber Ltd., 1945. 40p.

Included in the collection of Mumford's essays, *City Development* (1945), with the title "The Plan of London."

A20   *City Development; Studies in Disintegration and Renewal.*
New York: Harcourt, Brace and Co., 1945. 248p.

A21   *Values for Survival; Essays, Addresses, and Letters on Politics and Education.*
New York: Harcourt, Brace and Co., 1946. 314p.

A22   *Green Memories; The Story of Geddes Mumford.*
New York: Harcourt, Brace and Co., 1947. 342p.

A23   *Man as Interpreter.*
New York: Harcourt, Brace and Co., 1950. 17p.

". . . part of a section on the nature of man that forms an intro-duction to the main theme of *The Conduct of Life.*" From the author's preface.

Privately printed for the friends of the author and his publishers as a New Year's greeting for 1951.

A24 *The Conduct of Life.*
New York: Harcourt, Brace and Co., 1951. 342p.

Fourth and final volume in The Renewal of Life series.

Reprinted with the same title and published as follows:

New York: Harvest Books, Harcourt, Brace and Co., 1951. 342p.
Reprinted in this edition by Harcourt Brace Jovanovich in 1970, with a new preface by Lewis Mumford.

A25 *Toward a Free World: Long-Range Planning under Democratic Control.*
New York: Church Peace Union, 1952. 16p.

An address given at the Conference on World Order, Rochester, New York, November 13, 1951.

A26 *Art and Technics.*
Bampton Lectures in America, No. 4. New York: Columbia University Press, 1952. 162p.

Reprinted with the same title and published as follows:

New York: Columbia Paperback, Columbia University Press, 1960. 162p.

A27 *In the Name of Sanity.*
New York: Harcourt, Brace and Co., 1954. 244p.

A28 *The Human Prospect.*
Edited by Harry T. Moore and Karl W. Deutsch. Boston: Beacon Paperback, Beacon Press, 1955. 319p.

Reprinted with the same title and published as follows:

Carbondale: Arcturus Books, Southern Illinois University Press, 1965. 319p.

A29 *From the Ground Up; Observations on Contemporary Architecture, Housing, Highway Building, and Civic Design.*
New York: Harvest Books, Harcourt, Brace and Co., 1956. 243p.

An original paperback edition.

A30 *The Transformations of Man.*
World Perspectives, Vol. 7. New York: Harper & Bros., 1956. 249p.

Reprinted with the same title and published as follows:

New York: Collier Books, 1962. 188p.

A31 *The Human Way Out.*
Pendle Hill Pamphlet No. 97. Wallingford, Pa.: Pendle Hill, 1958. 28p.

Originally given as a speech at the closing of the Prayer and Conscience Vigil held in Washington, D.C., in November 1957.

A32 *The Role of the Creative Arts in Contemporary Society.*
Distinguished Lecture Series, Durham, N.H.: University of New Hampshire, 1958. 23p.

An address given at the University of New Hampshire, February 28, 1957.

First published in *Virginia Quarterly Review*, XXXIII (Fall 1957), 521–38.

A33 *The City in History: Its Origins, Its Transformations, and Its Prospects.*
New York: Harcourt, Brace and Co., 1961. 657p.

Reprinted with the same title and published as follows:

New York: Harbinger Books, Harcourt, Brace and World, 1961. 657p.

A34 *Social Responsibilities of the Business Community.*
Baltimore: Baltimore Life Insurance Co., 1961. 18p.

An address presented at the new home office building of the Baltimore Life Insurance Co., Baltimore, Maryland, April 24, 1961.

A35 *The Highway and the City.*
New York: Harvest Books, Harcourt, Brace and World, 1963. 246p.
An original paperback edition.

Reprinted with the same title and published as follows:

New York: Mentor Book, New American Library, 1964. 256p.

A36 *The Myth of the Machine: I. Technics and Human Development.*
New York: Harcourt, Brace and World, 1967. 342p.

This is the first volume of a two-volume work; the second volume published in 1970.

A37 *The Urban Prospect.*
New York: Harcourt, Brace and World, 1968. 255p.

Reprinted with the same title and published as follows:

New York: Harvest Books, Harcourt, Brace and World, 1968. 255p.

A38   *The Myth of the Machine: II. The Pentagon of Power.*
New York: Harcourt Brace Jovanovich, 1970. 496p.

This is the second volume of a two-volume work; the first volume published in 1967.

B. WRITINGS IN PERIODICALS

NOTE: The term "periodical," as I have used it, has a broad scope to include such publications as the proceedings of a society, association, or similar organization. This interpretation seemed preferable to scattering the citations over a number of categories in order to accommodate minor exceptions.

A special point needs to be made in regard to Mumford's articles published in the *New Yorker*. Thanks to Robert O. Johnson's *An Index to Literature in the 'New Yorker'; Volumes I–XV, 1925–1940*, I discovered that in the period from October 5, 1929, to April 2, 1960, the *New Yorker* was published in both a New York City edition and an Out-of-Town edition. Pagination is not always identical in the same issue of each edition; therefore, an article in the same issue may appear on different pages in each edition. Except for libraries in the New York City area, most libraries have mixed sets as the *New Yorker* did not make a careful distinction in mailing the two editions. And there is one further complicating factor: many of Mumford's articles, particularly in the early 1930's, appeared only in the New York City edition. These unfortunate quirks in publication should be kept in mind when referring to a citation to a *New Yorker* article published in the period mentioned above.

The reader should also note that, as often happens in magazine and newspaper publication, the titles are not necessarily those chosen by the author. Occasionally they give a false clue to the contents.

1914

B1   "Jones and I."
      Metropolitan; the Livest Magazine in America, XXXIX (February 1914), 13.

   Written in response to the magazine's offer of $1000 for the best letter answering George Bernard Shaw's article, "The Case for Equality," that had appeared in the December 1913 issue. Although Lincoln Steffens won the prize, the judges thought so well of Mumford's reply that it was the only other printed. Article signed Lewis C. Mumford.

B2   "Community Cooking."
     Forum, LII (July 1914), 95–99.

B3   "Fruit."
     Forum, LII (December 1914), 889–92.

     A short story.

1918

B4   "Napoleon and the Baltic Block."
     Public, A Journal of Democracy, XXI (April 13, 1918), 459–61.

B5   "The Marriage of Museums."
     Scientific Monthly, VII (September 1918), 252–60.

1919

B6   "Finland—A Bulwark against Bolshevism."
     Dial, LXVI (June 14, 1919), 590–92.

B7   "The Heritage of the Cities Movement in America; An Historical
        Survey."
     American Institute of Architects. Journal, VII (August 1919), 349–
     54.

B8   "Attacking the Housing Problem on Three Fronts."
     Nation, CIX (September 6, 1919), 332–33.

B9   "The Place of the Community in the School."
     Dial, LXVII (September 20, 1919), 244–46.

B10 "Wardom and the State."
     Dial, LXVII (October 4, 1919), 303–05.

1920

B11 "A Very Royal Academy."
     Freeman, I (June 16, 1920), 327–28.

B12 "Il Faut Cultiver Son Jardin."
     Freeman, I (July 7, 1920), 396–97.

B13 "The Tate Gallery Reopens."
     Freeman, II (September 22, 1920), 38–39.

B14 "The Adolescence of Reform."
     Freeman, II (December 1, 1920), 272–73.

B15 "Sociology and Its Prospects in Great Britain."
Athenaeum; A Journal of English and Foreign Literature, Science, the Fine Arts, Music, and the Drama, December 10, 1920, pp. 815–16.

B16 "Miscellany."
Freeman, II (December 15, 1920), 326–27.

Signed "Journeyman"; Mumford wrote only the first five paragraphs.

1921

B17 "Miscellany."
Freeman, II (January 26, 1921), 470–71.

Signed "Journeyman."

B18 "Miscellany."
Freeman, II (February 9, 1921), 517–18.

Signed "Journeyman"; Mumford's contribution ends with the second paragraph on page 518.

B19 "Towards a Humanist Synthesis."
Freeman, II (March 2, 1921), 583–85.

B20 "Miscellany."
Freeman, III (April 13, 1921), 110–11.

Signed "Journeyman."

B21 "Beauty and the Picturesque."
Freeman, III (July 13, 1921), 419–20.

See *Freeman,* IV (September 14, 1921), 17–18, for Mumford's reply to a critic of this article.

B22 "The Collapse of Tomorrow."
Freeman, III (July 13, 1921), 414–15.

An unsigned editorial.

B23 "The History of a Prodigy."
Smart Set, LXV (August 1921), 49–52.

A short story.

B24 "Miscellany."
Freeman, III (August 3, 1921), 495–96.

Signed "Journeyman."

B25   "Machinery and the Modern Style."
       New Republic, XXVII (August 3, 1921), 263–65.

       Included as a chapter in Lewis Mumford, ed., *Roots of Contemporary American Architecture* (1952, 1959).

B26   "The Wilderness of Suburbia."
       New Republic, XXVIII (September 7, 1921), 44–45.

B27   "Miscellany."
       Freeman, IV (September 21, 1921), 38–39.

       Signed "Journeyman."

B28   "Dulcy's World."
       Freeman, IV (November 2, 1921), 183–84.

       Dramatic criticism.

B29   " 'The Madras House.' "
       Freeman, IV (December 14, 1921), 328–29.

       Dramatic criticism.

B30   "Miscellany."
       Freeman, IV (December 14, 1921), 327–28.

       Signed "Journeyman."

       1922

B31   "Reeducating the Worker."
       Survey, XLVII (January 7, 1922), 567–69.

B32   "The Hebrew University: The Vision of the Architect."
       Menorah Journal, VIII (February 1922), 33–36.

B33   "Ex Libris."
       Freeman, IV (February 22, 1922), 574–75.

B34   "Abandoned Roads."
       Freeman, V (April 12, 1922), 101–02.

       An unsigned editorial. Included in *The Freeman Book*. New York: B. W. Huebsch, 1924.

B35   "Life by Rule of Thumb."
       Freeman, V (April 12, 1922), 102–03.

       An unsigned editorial.

B36   "Miscellany."
       Freeman, V (May 17, 1922), 231–32.

Signed "Journeyman."

B37 "Nationalism or Culturism? A Search for the True Community."
Menorah Journal, VIII (June 1922), 129–38.

B38 "England's American Summer."
Freeman, V (June 7, 1922), 296.

B39 "Americanized Europe."
Freeman, VI (November 22, 1922), 253–54.

1923

B40 "Wilt Thou Play with Leviathan?"
New Republic, XXXIII (January 24, 1923), 215–16.

An unsigned editorial.

B41 "The Architectural League's Exhibition."
American Institute of Architects. Journal, XI (March 1923), 111–13.

B42 "Neighbors."
Survey Graphic, L (April 1, 1923), 44.

A brief, unsigned sketch of Patrick Geddes who was coming to the United States in May 1923 for a visit.

B43 "Ex Libris."
Freeman, VII (April 18, 1923), 143; (April 25, 1923), 167; (May 2, 1923), 190–91.

B44 "The American Language."
Freeman, VII (May 16, 1923), 222–24.

An unsigned editorial.

B45 "Beauty and the Industrial Beast."
New Republic, XXXV (June 6, 1923), 37–38.

For a minor correction to this article, see same volume, issue of June 13, 1923, page 80.

B46 "New Trails for Old."
Freeman, VII (July 4, 1923), 396–97.

B47 "Architectural Piety."
American Institute of Architects. Journal, XI (August 1923), 304+.

B48 "Herzl's Utopia."
Menorah Journal, IX (August 1923), 155–69.

B49   "Regional Planning Schemes."
      American Institute of Architects. Journal, XI (October 1923), 404–
      05.

B50   "The Regional Note."
      Freeman, VIII (October 10, 1923), 107–08.

B51   "The Mood of Satire."
      Freeman, VIII (November 14, 1923), 224–25.

B52   "Community Planning and Housing."
      American Institute of Architects. Journal, XI (December 1923), 492.

B53   "American Architecture: The Medieval Tradition."
      Freeman, VIII (December 19, 1923), 344–46.

      This and the four subsequent articles in *Freeman* with the general
      title "American Architecture" make up the first five chapters, some-
      what expanded, in Mumford's *Sticks and Stones* (1924).

      1924

B54   "Our Modern Style."
      American Institute of Architects. Journal, XII (January 1924), 26–
      27.

B55   "American Architecture: The Heritage of the Renaissance."
      Freeman, VIII (January 2, 1924), 394–96.

B56   "American Architecture: The Classical Myth."
      Freeman, VIII (January 9, 1924), 418–20.

B57   "American Architecture: The Diaspora of the Pioneer."
      Freeman, VIII (February 13, 1924), 538–40.

B58   "American Architecture: The Realization of Industrialism."
      Freeman, VIII (February 27, 1924), 584–86.

B59   "Architecture and History."
      American Institute of Architects. Journal, XII (April 1924), 191–92.

B60   "Poe and an American Myth."
      Literary Review, IV (April 5, 1924), 641–42.

B61   " 'The New Poverty' in Architecture."
      American Institute of Architects. Journal, XII (July 1924), 332–33.

B62   "The Imperial Age."
      American Institute of Architects. Journal, XII (August 1924), 366–
      71.

For a correction to this article by Mumford, see same volume, issue of December 1924, page 539.

Included, with slight changes, as a chapter with the title "The Imperial Façade" in Mumford's *Sticks and Stones* (1924). Also included in the collection of Mumford's essays and other writings, *The Human Prospect* (1955).

B63   "Architecture and the Machine."
      American Mercury, III (September 1924), 77–80.

B64   "Devastated Regions."
      American Mercury, III (October 1924), 217–20.

      A fictional dialogue between a critic and his friend.

B65   "High Buildings: An American View."
      Architects' Journal, LX (October 1, 1924), 487.

      Also published in *American Architect*, CXXVI (November 5, 1924), 423–24.

B66   "Arms and the—Baby."
      New Republic, XL (October 15, 1924), 160–61.

      An unsigned editorial.

B67   "Aesthetics: A Palaver."
      American Mercury, III (November 1924), 360–65.

      A fictional dialogue among four friends; identifiable as Ernest Boyd, Van Wyck Brooks, Clarence Britten, and J. E. Spingarn, although Britten was not present.

      Published separately, under the author's original title, as *Aesthetics, A Dialogue*. Troutbeck Leaflets, No. 3. Amenia, New York: Privately printed at the Troutbeck Press, 1925. 14p.

B68   "Contemporary Disillusion; A Dialogue."
      Nation, CXIX (December 10, 1924), 636–37.

      A fictional conversation between a poet and a critic; identifiable as Babette Deutsch and Lewis Mumford respectively.

B69   "American Interiors."
      New Republic, XLI (December 31, 1924), 139–40.

B70   "Report of Committee on Community Planning."
      American Institute of Architects. *Proceedings of the Fifty-seventh Annual Convention* (1924), Appendix 6, pp. 120–26.

Although not a member of the Committee, Mumford wrote this report using data contributed by Committee members and further interpreted in discussions with them. The second report was presented in 1925.

1925

B71 "The Censor and Society."
Guardian, A Literary Monthly, January 1925, pp. 65–67.

B72 "Towers."
American Mercury, IV (February 1925), 193–96.

A fictional conversation between an architect and a critic.

B73 "Who *Is* Patrick Geddes?"
Survey Graphic, LIII (February 1, 1925), 523–24.

B74 "Houses—Sunnyside Up."
Nation, CXX (February 4, 1925), 115–16.

B75 "Architecture and Catholicism."
Commonweal, I (April 15, 1925), 623–25.

B76 "Community Planning and the Architect."
American Institute of Architects. *Proceedings of the Fifty-eighth Annual Convention* (1925), pp. 27–30.

An address delivered in New York City, April 21, 1925.

B77 "Report of Committee on Community Planning."
American Institute of Architects. *Proceedings of the Fifty-eighth Annual Convention* (1925), Appendix 10, pp. 119–26.

This is Part II of the report cited above presented to the 1924 Convention. Mumford drafted this report also.

B78 "Regions—To Live in."
Survey Graphic, LIV (May 1, 1925), 151–52.

B79 "The Fourth Migration."
Survey Graphic, LIV (May 1, 1925), 130–33.

Included as a preface to the collection of Mumford's essays, *The Urban Prospect* (1968).

B80 "Architecture and Broad Planning: Realities vs. Dreams."
American Institute of Architects. Journal, XIII (June 1925), 198–99.

B81   "Towards a Modern Synagogue Architecture."
Menorah Journal, XI (June 1925), 225–40.

B82   "The American Intelligentsia."
World Tomorrow, VIII (July 1925), 200–01.

B83   "The Architecture of Escape."
New Republic, XLIII (August 12, 1925), 321–22.

B84   "The Poison of Good Taste."
American Mercury, VI (September 1925), 92–94.

B85   "Decoration and Structure."
Commonweal, II (October 7, 1925), 532–33.

B86   "The Social Background of Frank Lloyd Wright."
Wendingen (Santpoort, Holland), VII (no. 5, 1925), 65–67+.

Also published with the same title in *The Life-Work of the American Architect, Frank Lloyd Wright*. Edited by Hendricus Th. Wijdeveld. Santpoort, Holland: C. A. Mees, 1925.

B87   "Die Form in der Amerikanischen Zivilisation."
Die Form, November 1925, pp. 25–29.

An original article.

B88   "The Emergence of a Past."
New Republic, XLV (November 25, 1925), 18–19.

B89   "Climax."
American Institute of Architects. Journal, XIII (December 1925), 454–56.

B90   "The Bricks of Baltimore."
Baltimore Evening Sun, Section 2 (December 1, 1925), p. 23.

Three other articles on Baltimore were published in this four-part series:

"Deserts versus Gardens."
Baltimore Evening Sun, Section 2 (December 4, 1925), p. 25.

"Modern Public Buildings."
Baltimore Evening Sun, Section 2 (December 8, 1925), p. 27.

"How to Ruin Baltimore."
Baltimore Evening Sun, Section 2 (December 10, 1925), p. 27.

1926

B91   "The Sacred City."
      New Republic, XLV (January 27, 1926), 270–71.

B92   "The Intolerable City; Must It Keep on Growing?"
      Harper's Magazine, CLII (February 1926), 283–93.

B93   "The New Municipal Building."
      Baltimore Evening Sun, Section 2 (February 11, 1926), p. 23.

B94   "The Destruction of the Shelton."
      Commonweal, III (April 28, 1926), 689–90.

B95   "Cities Old and New—The Culture Cycle and City Planning."
      American Institute of Architects. Journal, XIV (June 1926), 291–93.

B96   "Symbolic Architecture."
      American Mercury, VIII (June 1926), 183–86.

B97   "Science and Sanctity."
      Commonweal, IV (June 9, 1926), 126–28.

B98   "Fashions Change in Utopia."
      New Republic, XLVII (June 16, 1926), 114–15.

B99   "Radicalism Can't Die."
      Jewish Daily Forward (English section), June 20, 1926, p. 1+.

      One of the series on "What Is a Radical?" written by different
      authors.

B100 "The Child as Artist."
      New Republic, XLVII (June 30, 1926), 165–67.

B101 "Origins of the American Mind."
      American Mercury, VIII (July 1926), 345–54.

      Appears with some changes as Chapter One in Mumford's *The
      Golden Day* (1926).

      Included in the collection of Mumford's essays and other writings,
      The Human Prospect (1955).

B102 "Grub-Street Theaters."
      Theatre Arts Monthly, X (August 1926), 527–32.

B103 "After Dullness—What? A Miscellany of Brief Answers by People
         in Their Thirties."
      Survey Graphic, LVII (November 1, 1926), 182–83.

Mumford's article is entitled "Regionalism."

B104 "Brancusi and Marin."
New Republic, XLIX (December 15, 1926), 112–13.

B105 "Magnified Impotence."
New Republic, XLIX (December 22, 1926), 138–40.

1927

B106 "The Machine and Its Products."
American Mercury, X (January 1927), 64–67.

B107 "The Paralysis of Luxury."
Commonweal, V (January 5, 1927), 237–38.

B108 "The Moderns."
New Republic, XLIX (January 12, 1927), 221–22.

B109 "The Fate of Garden Cities."
American Institute of Architects. Journal, XV (February 1927), 37–39.

B110 "Is the Skyscraper Tolerable?"
Architecture (N.Y.), LV (February 1927), 67–69.

B111 "O'Keef[f]e and Matisse."
New Republic, L (March 2, 1927), 41–42.

B112 "A Modern Catholic Architect."
Commonweal, V (March 2, 1927), 458–59.

B113 "An American Epic in Paint."
New Republic, L (April 6, 1927), 197.

B114 "Blind Staggers."
New Masses, III (May 1927), 25.

B115 "The Heritage of Impressionism."
New Republic, L (May 18, 1927), 355–57.

B116 "The Next Twenty Years in City Planning."
National Conference on City Planning. Planning Problems of Town, City and Region. Papers and discussions at the 19th National Conference on City Planning held at Washington, D.C., May 9–11, 1927, pp. 45–58.

B117 "The Barclay-Vesey Building."
New Republic, LI (July 6, 1927), 176–77.

See vol. LII (August 24, 1927), 21, for a letter to the editor by Mumford with additional comments on the Barclay-Vesey Building.

B118 "That Monster—The Machine."
New Masses, III (September 1927), 23.

B119 "Regionalism and Irregionalism."
Sociological Review, XIX (October 1927), 277–88.

This article is one of a series, "The Theory and Practice of Regionalism," which is continued in vol. XX (January 1928), 18–33, and (April 1928), 131–41.

B120 "American Taste."
Harper's Magazine, CLV (October 1927), 569–77.

Published separately as *American Taste*. San Francisco: The Westgate Press, 1929. 33p.

B121 "Mid-American Reflections."
New Republic, LII (October 12, 1927), 208–09.

B122 "New York vs. Chicago in Architecture."
Architecture (N.Y.), LVI (November 1927), 241–44.

B123 "American Architecture."
American Federationist, XXXIV (December 1927), 1479–84.

1928

B124 "Modernist Furniture."
New Republic, LIV (March 21, 1928), 154–55.

B125 "American Architecture Today." Part 1
Architecture (N.Y.), LVII (April 1928), 181–88.

Part 2: LVII (June 1928), 301–08.

Part 3: LVIII (October 1928), 189–204.

B126 "Towards a Rational Modernism."
New Republic, LIV (April 25, 1928), 297–98.

B127 "Back to the Table."
New Republic, LV (August 15, 1928), 332–33.

B128 "Art in the Machine Age."
Saturday Review of Literature, V (September 8, 1928), 102–03.

Included in expanded form as a chapter entitled "The Arts" in

Charles A. Beard, ed., *Whither Mankind; A Panorama of Modern Civilization* (1928).

B129 "The Woman Who Did."
New Republic, LVI (September 19, 1928), 126–27.

B130 "The Significance of Herman Melville."
New Republic, LVI (October 10, 1928), 212–14.

This and the two articles immediately following are included with some changes in Mumford's *Herman Melville* (1929).

B131 "The Writing of *Moby Dick*."
American Mercury, XV (December 1928), 482–90.

B132 "Young Olympian."
Saturday Review of Literature, V (December 15, 1928), 514–15.

1929

B133 "Less Money and More Life: How to Make Your Income More Productive."
Harper's Magazine, CLVIII (January 1929), 158–67.

Written under the pseudonym "Raymond Essen."

B134 "The Economics of Contemporary Decoration."
Creative Art, IV (January 1929), 19–22.

B135 "Reflections on Chicago."
New Republic, LVIII (February 27, 1929), 44–45.

For Mumford's reply to criticism of this article, see same volume, issue of April 3, 1929, page 202.

B136 "On Judging Art."
New Republic, LVIII (March 20, 1929), 129–30.

Mumford replies to criticism of this article in the same volume, issue of April 10, 1929, page 229.

B137 "Modernism for Sale."
American Mercury, XVI (April 1929), 453–55.

B138 "Does America Discourage Art? A Socratic Dialogue."
Forum, LXXXI (April 1929), 232–37.

Mumford is one of the eleven participants in the dialogue.

B139 "Alfred Stieglitz, '84."
City College Alumnus (N.Y.), XXV (May 1929), 149–51.

B140 [Comments on Sacco and Vanzetti Case.]
Lantern; Focusing upon Fascism and Other Dark Disorders of the Day, August 1929, pp. 6–7.

B141 "From a Country Notebook."
New Republic, LIX (August 7, 1929), 313.

B142 "Form in Modern Architecture." Part I: "The Breakup of Form."
Architecture (N.Y.), LX (September 1929), 125–28.

This first part reprinted in *Sociological Review*, XXII (October 1930), 329–33.

Part II: "The Beginnings of Modern Form." LX (December 1929), 313–16.

Part III: "The Social Contribution." LXI (March 1930), 151–53.

Part IV: "The Community as a Source of Form." LXII (July 1930), 1–4.

Part V: "The Wavy Line Versus the Cube." LXII (December 1930), 315–18.

This final part reprinted in *Architectural Record*, CXXXV (January 1964), 111–16.

B143 "From a City Notebook."
New Republic, LX (September 18, 1929), 125–26.

B144 "Botched Cities."
American Mercury, XVIII (October 1929), 143–50.

B145 "Patrick Geddes, Insurgent."
New Republic, LX (October 30, 1929), 295–96.

For a minor correction, see Mumford's letter to the editor in vol. LXI (November 20, 1929), 377.

Included with a 1936 postscript in *The New Republic Anthology*. New York: Dodge Publishing Co., 1936.

1930
B146 "Mass-Production and the Modern House."
Architectural Record, LXVII (January 1930), 13–20; (February 1930), 110–16.

Included in the collection of Mumford's essays, *City Development* (1945), with the title "Mass-Production and Housing."

B147 "The Booby Prizes for 1929."
New Republic, LXI (January 8, 1930), 190–91.

Mumford replies to criticism of this article in the same volume, issue of February 5, 1930, page 304.

B148 "The Buried Renaissance."
New Freeman, I (March 15, 1930), 12–13.

B149 "The American Dwelling-House."
American Mercury, XIX (April 1930), 469–77.

B150 "A Modern Synthesis."
Saturday Review of Literature, VI (April 12, 1930), 920–21; (May
10, 1930), 1028–29.

Included, in somewhat altered form, with the title "Towards an
Organic Humanism" in *The Critique of Humanism.* Edited by
C. Hartley Grattan. New York: Brewer and Warren, 1930.

B151 "American Condescension and European Superiority."
Scribner's Magazine, LXXXVII (May 1930), 518–27.

B152 "The Drama of the Machines."
Scribner's Magazine, LXXXVIII (August 1930), 150–61.

B153 "Victor Branford."
New Republic, LXIV (August 27, 1930), 43–44.

Reprinted with a few additions from a letter to Patrick Geddes under the title "Victor Branford, A Brave Fine Spirit" in *Sociological
Review,* XXIII (January 1931), 7–11.

B154 "The Chance for Civilized Housing."
New Republic, LXIV (September 17, 1930), 115–17.

B155 "The Image of Randolph Bourne."
New Republic, LXIV (September 24, 1930), 151–52.

B156 "Publishing, Old and New."
New Republic, LXIV (October 1, 1930), 176–78.

B157 "What I Believe."
Forum, LXXXIV (November 1930), 263–68.

Included in different form in *Living Philosophies.* New York: Simon and Schuster, 1931.

B158 "A Challenge to American Intellectuals: A Controversy. The Evolutionary Approach."
Modern Quarterly, V (Winter 1930–31), 407–10.

1931

B159 "The America of Sinclair Lewis."
Current History, XXXIII (January 1931), 529–33.

Included in *Sinclair Lewis: A Collection of Critical Essays*. Edited by Mark Schorer. Englewood Cliffs, N.J.: Prentice-Hall, 1962.

B160 "Prelude to the Present."
New York Herald Tribune Books, January 11, 1931, p. 1+.

B161 "The Mood of a Decade."
New York Herald Tribune Books, January 18, 1931, p. 1+.

B162 "Two Chicago Fairs."
New Republic, LXV (January 21, 1931), 271–72.

B163 "Predicament of Emptiness."
New York Herald Tribune Books, January 25, 1931, p. 1+.

B164 "The Brown Decades."
Scribner's Magazine, LXXXIX (February 1931), 135–44; (April 1931), 385–95; XC (October 1931), 361–72.

B165 "Autopsy upon an Immortal."
New York Herald Tribune Books, February 8, 1931, p. 1+.

Through a newspaper printing error, this article was given the title intended for a book review on the same page. The correct title is "The Birth of Order."

B166 "Notes on Modern Architecture."
New Republic, LXVI (March 18, 1931), 119–22.

Mumford responds to criticism of this article in the same volume, issue of May 6, 1931, page 331.

B167 "Fifty Prints."
Art Digest, V (April 1, 1931), 19–20+.

Mumford's choice of the "Fifty Prints of the Year."

B168 "The Flaw in the Mechanical House."
New Republic, LXVII (June 3, 1931), 65-66.

Mumford's reply to criticism of this article appears in this same volume, issue of July 8, 1931, pages 208–10.

B169 "Frozen Music or Solidified Static? Reflections on Radio City."
New Yorker, VII (June 20, 1931), 28+.

B170 "The Brooklyn Bridge."
American Mercury, XXIII (August 1931), 447–50.

B171 "Thorstein Veblen."
New Republic, LXVII (August 5, 1931), 314–16.

B172 "A Footnote to a Decade."
New York Herald Tribune Books, August 9, 1931, p. 1+.

B173 "Contemporary Industrial Art."
New Yorker, VII (November 14, 1931), p. 36+.

B174 "The Sky Line: Bridges and Buildings."
New Yorker, VII (November 21, 1931), 82.

B175 "If I Were a Dictator."
Nation, CXXXIII (December 9, 1931), 631–33.

B176 "The Sky Line: The Modern Hospital."
New Yorker, VII (December 12, 1931), 48+.

B177 "Housing versus Ownership."
New Republic, LXIX (December 16, 1931), 122–23.

An unsigned editorial.

1932

B178 "The Sky Line: From the Palace of the Popes; The Cantilevered Front; Return to Sobriety."
New Yorker, VII (January 2, 1932), 43–44.

B179 "The Sky Line: Unconscious Architecture."
New Yorker, VII (February 13, 1932), 46+.

B180 "The Sky Line: Organic Architecture."
New Yorker, VIII (February 27, 1932), 45–46.

B181 "The Sky Line: A Survivor of the Brown Decades; De Mortuis; What Might Have Been."
New Yorker, VIII (March 19, 1932), 71–72.

B182 "The Sky Line: Medals and Mentions."
New Yorker, VIII (April 16, 1932), p. 36+.

B183 "The Sky Line: The Regional Plan."
New Yorker, VIII (May 21, 1932), 64–66.

B184 "The Plan of New York."
New Republic, LXXI (June 15, 1932), 121–26; (June 22, 1932), 146–54.

B185 "The Sky Line: On Making a Museum; Post-Boom Tower; The Modern Restaurant."
New Yorker, VIII (June 25, 1932), 50–52.

B186 "The Art Galleries: The Taste of Today."
New Yorker, VIII (October 1, 1932), 56–58.

B187 "The Art Galleries: Shows Abroad."
New Yorker, VIII (October 8, 1932), 35–37.

B188 "The Art Galleries: Mr. Bloom's Anniversary; And a Disciple of Atget."
New Yorker, VIII (October 15, 1932), 65–66.

B189 "The Sky Line: Gas Tanks and Towers; The New Architect."
New Yorker, VIII (October 22, 1932), 30+.

B190 "Notes on Germany."
New Republic, LXXII (October 26, 1932), 279–81.

B191 "The Art Galleries: The Coleman Memorial; Frescoes from Persia."
New Yorker, VIII (October 29, 1932), 53.

B192 "England's Two Million Houses, New. Housing in England."
Fortune, VI (November 1932), 32–37+.

B193 "The Art Galleries: On Talent and Success; Statues without Frames."
New Yorker, VIII (November 5, 1932), 36.

B194 "The Art Galleries: Seventy Years; The Work of Mary Cassatt."
New Yorker, VIII (November 12, 1932), 63–64.

B195 "The Art Galleries: Marin; Miró."
New Yorker, VIII (November 19, 1932), 69–70.

B196 "The Sky Line: The Laundry Takes to Architecture."
New Yorker, VIII (November 26, 1932), 36–37.

B197 "In Our Stars. The World Fifty Years from Now."
Forum, LXXXVIII (December 1932), 338–42.

B198 "What Has 1932 Done for Literature?"
Atlantic Monthly, CL (December 1932), 761–67.

B199 "The Art Galleries: The Metropolitan Shows a Bequest;
Abstraction; Sculpturesque Glass."
New Yorker, VIII (December 3, 1932), 79–80.

B200 "The Art Galleries: American Painting."
New Yorker, VIII (December 10, 1932), 46.

B201 "The Art Galleries: Assorted Americana."
New Yorker, VIII (December 17, 1932), 62.

B202 "The Art Galleries: Black-and-White; The Realism of
Bouguereau."
New Yorker, VIII (December 24, 1932), 39.

1933

B203 "The Art Galleries: The Rockefeller Collection."
New Yorker, VIII (January 7, 1933), 45+.

B204 "The Sky Line: Two Theatres."
New Yorker, VIII (January 14, 1933), 55–56.

B205 "The Sky Line: Paint and Stone."
New Yorker, VIII (January 21, 1933), 48–49.

B206 "The Art Galleries: The Return of Good Painting; Surréaliste."
New Yorker, VIII (January 28, 1933), 33+.

B207 "Machines for Living."
Fortune, VII (February 1933), 78–80+.

B208 "The Art Galleries: Young Promises; The Working-Class Scene."
New Yorker, VIII (February 11, 1933), 53–54.

B209 "The Art Galleries: World Tour."
New Yorker, IX (February 18, 1933), 32.

B210 "Notes on North Sea Architecture."
Yale Review, new series, XXII (March 1933), 513–24.

B211 "The Sky Line: The Architects Show Their Wares."
New Yorker, IX (March 4, 1933), 53–54.

B212 "The Art Galleries: Sterne in Retrospect; Variations by Derain."
New Yorker, IX (March 11, 1933), 42–43.

B213 "The Art Galleries: Flora and Fauna; Two Sculptors; Monsieur
     Roy Makes a Joke."
     New Yorker, IX (March 25, 1933), 43.

B214 "The Art Galleries: Cabarets and Clouds."
     New Yorker, IX (April 1, 1933), 34–35.

B215 "The Art Galleries: Pulse of the Country; Local Color; A Word of
     Warning."
     New Yorker, IX (April 15, 1933), 53.

B216 "The Art Galleries: Impressionism and the Circus; Three Decades."
     New Yorker, IX (April 22, 1933), 28.

B217 "Taxes into Houses."
     Fortune, VII (May 1933), 48–49+.

B218 "The Art Galleries: Resurrection; And the Younger Generation."
     New Yorker, IX (May 13, 1933), 60.

B219 "Breaking the Housing Blockade!"
     New Republic, LXXV (May 17, 1933), 8–11.

     Mumford's reply to criticism of this article appears in the same vol-
     ume, issue of June 7, 1933, page 103.

B220 "The Art Galleries: Early Americans; Ben Shahn and Tom
     Mooney; Mr. Rivera's Mural."
     New Yorker, IX (May 20, 1933), 64–66.

B221 "The Sky Line: Skyscrapers and Tenements."
     New Yorker, IX (June 3, 1933), 36–38.

B222 "The Art Galleries: The Summer Circuit."
     New Yorker, IX (August 12, 1933), 26+.

B223 "The Art Galleries: West, South, and Across the Harlem."
     New Yorker, IX (September 23, 1933), 47–48+.

B224 "The Art Galleries: Fall Fashions; The Wives Put on a Show."
     New Yorker, IX (September 30, 1933), 40.

B225 "The Need for Concrete Goals."
     Common Sense, II (October 1933), 10–11.

B226 "The Sky Line: Beer and Grass; The Big Boys Turn Modern."
     New Yorker, IX (October 7, 1933), 48–50.

B227 "The Art Galleries: Anti-Graphic Photographs; Kent, Hale, and Orozco."
New Yorker, IX (October 14, 1933), 48–50.

B228 "The Art Galleries: Miniatures and Heirlooms."
New Yorker, IX (October 21, 1933), 38–40.

B229 "The Art Galleries: Extramural Activities."
New Yorker, IX (October 28, 1933), 42–44.

B230 "The Sky Line: Portholes on the Avenue; Bankers and Goldfish."
New Yorker, IX (November 4, 1933), 40+.

B231 "The Art Galleries: Two Americans."
New Yorker, IX (November 11, 1933), 60–61.

B232 "The Art Galleries: Giants, Past and Present."
New Yorker, IX (November 18, 1933), 42–44.

B233 "The Art Galleries: New York Under Glass."
New Yorker, IX (November 25, 1933), 50–52.

B234 "The Art Galleries: The Frozen Nightmares of Señor Dali."
New Yorker, IX (December 9, 1933), 56+.

B235 "The Art Galleries: Questions and Answers."
New Yorker, IX (December 16, 1933), 79.

B236 "The Sky Line: Mr. Rockefeller's Center."
New Yorker, IX (December 23, 1933), 29–30.

B237 "The Art Galleries: Across the Hudson; Jean Lurçat's Double Bill; Paints, Pastels, and the Parthenon."
New Yorker, IX (December 30, 1933), 31–32.

1934

B238 "The Task of Modern Biography."
English Journal, XXIII (January 1934), 1–9.

B239 "The Art Galleries: Rivera and the Workers."
New Yorker, IX (January 13, 1934), 32+.

B240 "The Art Galleries: Concerning Mr. Speicher; Two Alumni from the 'Masses'; Old Buildings and Young Ladies."
New Yorker, IX (January 20, 1934), 30–31.

B241 "The Art Galleries: Plays without Actors."
New Yorker, IX (January 27, 1934), 58.

B242 "The Art Galleries: Solidity and Sentiment; The Tragic Muse of
       Mr. Brook; Primitive."
       New Yorker, IX (February 3, 1934), 34+.

B243 "The Art Galleries: Sacred and Profane."
       New Yorker, IX (February 10, 1934), 47–49.

B244 "The Sky Line: Modernism and Mr. Mulrooney; Palaces in Black
       and White."
       New Yorker, X (February 17, 1934), 34+.

B245 "The Art Galleries: Statues and Gouaches; Portraits of Decay."
       New Yorker, X (February 24, 1934), 48–50.

B246 "New Homes for a New Deal." Part III: "The Shortage of
       Dwellings and Direction."
       New Republic, LXXVIII (February 28, 1934), 69–72.

B247 "New Homes for a New Deal." Part IV: "A Concrete Program."
       New Republic, LXXVIII (March 7, 1934), 91–94.

       Written by Mumford, in collaboration with Albert Mayer and
       Henry Wright, who also signed it.

B248 "The Art Galleries: Maurice Prendergast."
       New Yorker, X (March 17, 1934), 81.

B249 "The Art Galleries: Sculptor-Blacksmith; The French Tradition;
       Colors and Cubism."
       New Yorker, X (March 24, 1934), 59–61.

B250 "The Art Galleries: Portrait of the Mechanic as a Young Man;
       Newcomers in Retrospect."
       New Yorker, X (March 31, 1934), 32+.

B251 "The Art Galleries: Circus Time; Statues and Prints; Americana."
       New Yorker, X (April 7, 1934), 60+.

B252 "The Art Galleries: Memorials and Moderns."
       New Yorker, X (April 14, 1934), 61+.

B253 "The Art Galleries: Benton of Missouri; A Galaxy of Goyas."
       New Yorker, X (April 21, 1934), 55–57.

B254 "The Art Galleries: Toyshop; Reflections on Mediocrity."
       New Yorker, X (April 28, 1934), 64–66.

B255 "The Art Galleries: Surprise Party; Wit in Water Colors."
       New Yorker, X (May 5, 1934), 56+.

B256 "The Art Galleries: Bottom of the Bottle."
New Yorker, X (May 12, 1934), 62+.

B257 "The Sky Line: The New York Lunchroom."
New Yorker, X (May 19, 1934), 44+.

B258 "The Art Galleries: Tips for Travellers; The Modern Museum."
New Yorker, X (June 9, 1934), 48.

B259 "The Sky Line: On an Incinerator; Renovated Brownstone."
New Yorker, X (September 15, 1934), 75–77.

B260 "The Art Galleries: Critics and Cameras."
New Yorker, X (September 29, 1934), 33–35.

B261 "Orozco in New England."
New Republic, LXXX (October 10, 1934), 231–35.

B262 "The Art Galleries: A Catalogue and Homer."
New Yorker, X (October 20, 1934), 36+.

B263 "The Art Galleries: Modes and Moderns."
New Yorker, X (November 3, 1934), 48–50.

B264 "The Art Galleries: Romanticism."
New Yorker, X (November 10, 1934), 52+.

B265 "The Art Galleries: In Memoriam."
New Yorker, X (November 17, 1934), 34+.

B266 "The Art Galleries: Marin and Others."
New Yorker, X (November 24, 1934), 48+.

B267 "The Sky Line: Modern Design; And the New Bryant Park."
New Yorker, X (December 1, 1934), 48+.

B268 "The Art Galleries: Americans and Others."
New Yorker, X (December 8, 1934), 83–86.

B269 "The Art Galleries: A Camera and Alfred Stieglitz."
New Yorker, X (December 22, 1934), 30+.

B270 "A New York Childhood; Ta-Ra-Ra-Boom-De-Ay."
New Yorker, X (December 22, 1934), 18–23.
Signed L.M.

1935

B271 "The Sky Line: Meditations on a Zoo."
New Yorker, X (January 5, 1935), 50.

B272 "The Art Galleries: Sweet Grapes and Bitter Tea."
      New Yorker, X (January 12, 1935), 62–63.

B273 "The Art Galleries: Americans and Americana."
      New Yorker, X (January 19, 1935), 60–61.

B274 "The Art Galleries: Platitudes in Paint; Charm and Humanity; The
      Jokes of Miró."
      New Yorker, X (January 26, 1935), 50+.

B275 "The Art Galleries: Anniversary; Post-Centenary Whistler; Mr.
      Curry and the American Scene."
      New Yorker, X (February 2, 1935), 33–34.

B276 "The Art Galleries: Lachaise and O'Keeffe."
      New Yorker, X (February 9, 1935), 38–39.

B277 "The Art Galleries: Paints, Palettes, and the Public Wall."
      New Yorker, XI (February 16, 1935), 44+.

B278 "The Art Galleries: New High in Abstractions."
      New Yorker, XI (March 2, 1935), 37–39.

B279 "The Art Galleries: Depression Week."
      New Yorker, XI (March 9, 1935), 58–60.

B280 "The Sky Line: Bars and Lounges."
      New Yorker, XI (March 16, 1935), 81.

B281 "The Art Galleries: Spring and Renoir."
      New Yorker, XI (March 23, 1935), 30–32.

B282 "The Art Galleries: The Dark Continent; And George Grosz."
      New Yorker, XI (March 30, 1935), 69.

B283 "The Art Galleries: Mirrors and the Metropolitan."
      New Yorker, XI (April 6, 1935), 79–80.

B284 "The Art Galleries: The Three Bentons."
      New Yorker, XI (April 20, 1935), 48+.

B285 "The Sky Line: Mr. Wright's City; Downtown Dignity."
      New Yorker, XI (April 27, 1935), 63–65.

B286 "The Art Galleries: A Group of Americans."
      New Yorker, XI (May 4, 1935), 28+.

B287 "The Art Galleries: Portraits in Plaster."
      New Yorker, XI (May 18, 1935), 53–55.

B288 "When America Goes to War."
Modern Monthly, IX (June 1935), 203–04.

A symposium.

B289 "The Art Galleries: In Capitulation."
New Yorker, XI (June 1, 1935), 57.

B290 "Anniversary Postbag."
Yale Review, new series, XXV (September 1935), 23–25.

B291 "The Sky Line: Menageries and Piers."
New Yorker, XI (October 12, 1935), 62–63.

B292 "The Art Galleries: Léger and the Machine."
New Yorker, XI (October 19, 1935), 73–74.

B293 "The Art Galleries: A Synopsis of Ryder."
New Yorker, XI (November 2, 1935), 69–70.

B294 "The Sky Line: A Park with a View; M. Le Corbusier; Indians and
Platters."
New Yorker, XI (November 9, 1935), 73–74.

B295 "The Art Galleries: The Work of van Gogh."
New Yorker, XI (November 16, 1935), 81–82.

B296 "The Art Galleries: The French Eighteenth Century."
New Yorker, XI (November 30, 1935), 67–68.

B297 "The Social Significance of Contemporary Art."
*Social Frontier; A Journal of Educational Criticism and Reconstruc-
tion*, II (December 1935), 75–78.

B298 "The Sky Line: The New Housing."
New Yorker, XI (December 7, 1935), 105–06.

For Mumford's reply to criticism of this article, see same volume,
issue of January 4, 1936, pages 51–52.

B299 "The Art Galleries: Leaves from a Notebook."
New Yorker, XI (December 14, 1935), 96–97.

B300 "The Art Galleries: Fifth Avenue's New Museum."
New Yorker, XI (December 28, 1935), 41–42.

1936

B301 "The Sky Line: Old and New."
New Yorker, XI (January 11, 1936), 36+.

B302 "The Art Galleries: Autobiographies in Print."
New Yorker, XI (January 18, 1936), 48–49.

B303 "The Art Galleries: Group Shows and Solos."
New Yorker, XI (January 25, 1936), 45–46.

B304 "The Art Galleries: Goya, Homer, and Jones."
New Yorker, XI (February 8, 1936), 58–59.

B305 "The Art Galleries: William Gropper and an Open Letter."
New Yorker, XI (February 15, 1936), 59–61.

B306 "The Sky Line: Fiftieth Anniversary; A Georgian Post Office."
New Yorker, XII (February 29, 1936), 40–41.

B307 "The Art Galleries: Paint, Stone, and Technics."
New Yorker, XII (March 7, 1936), 57–58.

B308 "The Art Galleries: The Course of Abstraction."
New Yorker, XII (March 21, 1936), 61–62.

B309 "Technics, Capitalism, and Social Interpretation."
Journal of Social Philosophy, I (April 1936), 289–92.

B310 "The Art Galleries: Tourist in Tahiti; Hartl and Hartley; Spring
    Miscellany."
New Yorker, XII (April 4, 1936), 49–51.

B311 "The Sky Line: Concerning Glass Houses."
New Yorker, XII (April 11, 1936), 49–50.

B312 "The Art Galleries: French Tapestries; Assorted Americans."
New Yorker, XII (April 18, 1936), 60–61.

B313 "The Art Galleries: The Independent Show."
New Yorker, XII (May 2, 1936), 43–45.

B314 "The Art Galleries: Drawings and Illustrations; Pictures for the
    Public."
New Yorker, XII (May 16, 1936), 43–45.

B315 "The Sky Line: On Shops and Such."
New Yorker, XII (May 30, 1936), 48–49.

B316 "The Art Galleries: Looking Backward, Looking Forward."
New Yorker, XII (June 6, 1936), 29.

B317 "The Sky Line: Houses and Fairs."
New Yorker, XII (June 20, 1936), 31–32.

B318 "Henry Wright."
New Republic, LXXXVII (July 29, 1936), 348–50.

Included in the collection of Mumford's essays and other writings, *The Human Prospect* (1955).

B319 "The Art Galleries: East and West."
New Yorker, XII (September 26, 1936), 57–58.

B320 "The Sky Line: Modernity and Commerce."
New Yorker, XII (October 3, 1936), 39–40.

B321 "Art and the State—[Part] V. America."
Listener, XVI (October 7, 1936), 649–52.

B322 "The Art Galleries: The Treasury's Murals."
New Yorker, XII (October 17, 1936), 70–71.

B323 "The Sky Line: Parks and Playgrounds; New Buildings for Old."
New Yorker, XII (October 24, 1936), 36–38.

B324 "The Art Galleries: John Marin."
New Yorker, XII (October 31, 1936), 53–54.

B325 "Onward and Upward with the Arts: The Ready-Made House."
New Yorker, XII (November 7, 1936), 61–64.

B326 "The Art Galleries: Pablo Picasso."
New Yorker, XII (November 14, 1936), 107–09.

B327 "The Art Galleries: Some Contemporaries."
New Yorker, XII (November 21, 1936), 72–73.

B328 "The Art Galleries: Moderns: Assorted."
New Yorker, XII (November 28, 1936), 68–71.

B329 "The Art Galleries: On Reproductions."
New Yorker, XII (December 12, 1936), 91–93.

B330 "The Art Galleries: Surrealism and Civilization."
New Yorker, XII (December 19, 1936), 76–79.

Included in the collection of Mumford's essays and other writings, *The Human Prospect* (1955).

B331 "The Art Galleries: Winslow Homer."
New Yorker, XII (December 26, 1936), 34–36.

B332 "Letter to the President."
New Republic, LXXXIX (December 30, 1936), 263–65.

On maintaining the Works Progress Administration (WPA) Arts Project.

1937

B333 "The Sky Line: The City of the Future."
New Yorker, XII (January 9, 1937), 59–60.

B334 "The Art Galleries: The New Year."
New Yorker, XII (January 16, 1937), 47–48.

B335 "The Art Galleries: In Retrospect."
New Yorker, XII (January 30, 1937), 54–55.

B336 "The Art Galleries: Wood and Stone."
New Yorker, XII (February 13, 1937), 54–57.

B337 "The Art Galleries: The Life of the City."
New Yorker, XIII (February 27, 1937), 32+.

B338 "The Sky Line: Penguins and Architects."
New Yorker, XIII (March 6, 1937), 59–60.

B339 "The Art Galleries: Spring, Circuses, and Sport."
New Yorker, XIII (March 13, 1937), 71–72.

B340 "The Art Galleries: Satirist into Painter; A Centenary; Potpourri."
New Yorker, XIII (March 27, 1937), 48–49.

B341 "The Art Galleries: Prints and Paints."
New Yorker, XIII (April 3, 1937), 67–69.

B342 "The Art Galleries: Academicians and Others."
New Yorker, XIII (April 10, 1937), 48–51.

B343 "The Sky Line: Buildings and Books."
New Yorker, XIII (April 17, 1937), 39–40.

B344 "The Art Galleries: A Congress of Americans."
New Yorker, XIII (May 1, 1937), 53.

B345 "The Sky Line: The World's Fair."
New Yorker, XIII (May 8, 1937), 32–33.

B346 "The Art Galleries: Pierre-Auguste Renoir."
New Yorker, XIII (June 5, 1937), 34–37.

Included in the collection of Mumford's essays and other writings, *The Human Prospect* (1955).

B347 "The Sky Line: Plus and Minus."
New Yorker, XIII (June 19, 1937), 58–59.

B348 "The Sky Line: Bridges and Beaches."
New Yorker, XIII (July 17, 1937), 50–52.

B349 "The Sky Line: Gardens and Glass."
New Yorker, XIII (October 16, 1937), 68–70.

B350 "What Is a City?"
Architectural Record, LXXXII (November 1937), 58–62.

B351 "The Sky Line: New Façades."
New Yorker, XIII (November 20, 1937), 80–82.

B352 "A New York Adolescence: Tennis, Quadratic Equations, and
Love."
New Yorker, XIII (December 4, 1937), 86–94.

Included in the collection of Mumford's essays and other writings,
The Human Prospect (1955).

1938

B353 "Survey and Plan as Communal Education."
Social Frontier, IV (January 1938), 108–10.

This is a section from Mumford's *The Culture of Cities* (1938).

B354 "The Sky Line: For the Common Good."
New Yorker, XIII (January 8, 1938), 50–52.

B355 "The Sky Line: At Home, Indoors and Out."
New Yorker, XIII (February 12, 1938), 31.

B356 "The Sky Line: The New Order."
New Yorker, XIV (February 26, 1938), 36–37.

B357 "The Beginnings of Privacy."
Saturday Review of Literature, XVII (March 19, 1938), 6.

A short excerpt from Mumford's *The Culture of Cities* (1938).

B358 "The Sky Line: Chairs and Shops."
New Yorker, XIV (April 9, 1938), 61–62.

B359 "The Sky Line: The Golden Age in the West and the South."
New Yorker, XIV (April 30, 1938), 50–51.

B360 "Call to Arms."

New Republic, XCV (May 18, 1938), 39–42.
Mumford answers critics of this article in the same volume, issue of June 1, 1938, pages 103–04; issue of June 8, 1938, page 133; and issue of June 15, 1938, page 161.

Included in the collection of Mumford's essays, *Values for Survival* (1946), with material written for but not printed in the original article.

B361 "The Sky Line: Pax in Urbe."
New Yorker, XIV (May 21, 1938), 60–63.

B362 "Regional Survey for Citizenship."
University of the State of New York. Bulletin, no. 1143 (July 1, 1938), 37–47.

B363 "The Sky Line: Notes on Modernism."
New Yorker, XIV (October 22, 1938), 73–74.

B364 "The Sky Line: Dialectical House; The New Shops."
New Yorker, XIV (November 19, 1938), 48+.

B365 "The Future of the American City."
St. Louis Post-Dispatch. Sixtieth Anniversary section, December 11, 1938, pp. 7–8.

B366 "Books That Changed Our Minds."
New Republic, XCVII (December 21, 1938), 205.

A short list of eight books and a few comments.

B367 "The Sky Line: Bauhaus."
New Yorker, XIV (December 31, 1938), 38–40.

1939
B368 "Menorah Anniversary Dinner; Message."
Menorah Journal, XXVII (January–March 1939), 100–01.

B369 " 'The Decline of the West.' "
New Republic, XCVII (January 11, 1939), 275–79.

Mumford's essay in the series "Books That Changed Our Minds."

See vol. XCVIII (March 15, 1939), 169, for Mumford's reply to a critic of this article.

This essay, somewhat expanded, included in *Books That Changed Our Minds*. Edited by Malcolm Cowley and Bernard Smith. New York: Doubleday, Doran and Co., 1939.

B370 "Good Will Must Act."
Fight for Peace and Democracy, VI (February 1939), 22–23+.

B371 "The Sky Line: Westward Ho!"
New Yorker, XV (February 25, 1939), 44–46.

B372 "America at Armageddon."
Current History, L (March 1939), 24–25+.

B373 "Fascism Is Worse Than War."
Common Sense, VIII (March 1939), 10–11.

B374 "The Sky Line: The American Tradition."
New Yorker, XV (March 11, 1939), 47–48.

B375 "Reflections on Modern Architecture."
Twice A Year, II (Spring–Summer 1939), 135–41.

B376 "The Sky Line: Growing Pains; The New Museum."
New Yorker, XV (June 3, 1939), 40–42.

B377 "The Sky Line in Flushing: West Is East."
New Yorker, XV (June 17, 1939), 37–41.

Reprinted in *Royal Architectural Institute of Canada. Journal*, XVI (August 1939), 181–83.

B378 "America and the Next War."
New Republic, XCIX (June 28, 1939), 209.

A brief paragraph in response to a questionnaire from the *New Republic* editors.

B379 "The Sky Line in Flushing: Genuine Bootleg."
New Yorker, XV (July 29, 1939), 38–41.

B380 "The City, A World's Fair Film."
Architectural Review, LXXXVI (August 1939), 93–94.

Excerpts from Mumford's commentary which accompanied the film entitled *The City*. A complete description of this film is included in the section of this bibliography titled Other Works.

B381 "Scholar and Gentleman."
Saturday Review of Literature, XX (August 5, 1939), 8–9.

On the death of Joel Elias Spingarn.

Included in the collection of Mumford's essays and other writings, *The Human Prospect* (1955), with the title "J. E. Spingarn."

B382 "The Sky Line: New Faces on the Avenue."
New Yorker, XV (September 9, 1939), 58–59.

B383 "The Sky Line: Modern Housing, from A to X."
New Yorker, XV (October 28, 1939), 57–58.

B384 "Whither the City?"
American City, LIV (November 1939), 60–62.

An excerpt from Mumford's book *Whither Honolulu?* (1938).

B385 "The Menace to the American Promise."
New Republic, CI (November 8, 1939), 64–65.

B386 "The Sky Line: Shade and Sunlight."
New Yorker, XV (December 2, 1939), 73–75.

B387 "The Sky Line: Millions for Mausoleums."
New Yorker, XV (December 30, 1939), 45–46.

B388 "Fantasia on Time."
New Yorker, XV (December 30, 1939), 16.

A poem taken from Mumford's unfinished novel in verse, *Victor*.

Included in the collection of Mumford's essays and other writings, *The Human Prospect* (1955).

1940

B389 "Looking Forward."
American Philosophical Society. *Proceedings*, LXXXIII (no. 4, 1940), 539–47.

An address given April 19, 1940, in the "Symposium on Characteristics of American Culture and Its Place in General Culture."

B390 "Social Purposes and New Plans."
Survey Graphic, XXIX (February 1940), 119–21+.

B391 "The Sky Line: Versailles for the Millions."
New Yorker, XVI (February 17, 1940), 41–42.

B392 "The Sky Line: The Dead Past and the Dead Present."
New Yorker, XVI (March 23, 1940), 54–55.

B393 "The Corruption of Liberalism."
New Republic, CII (April 29, 1940), 568–73.

Republished in the 40th Anniversary issue of *New Republic*, CXXXI (November 22, 1954), 93–97.

Included, in a revised and expanded form, in the collection of Mumford's essays, *Faith for Living* (1940), chapters 9–19.

In a further revised and shorter form included in the collection of Mumford's essays, *Values for Survival* (1946).

B394 "The Sky Line: Rockefeller Center Revisited."
New Yorker, XVI (May 4, 1940), 73–74.

B395 "Thomas Beer, Aristocrat of Letters."
Saturday Review of Literature, XXII (May 4, 1940), 3–4+.

B396 "U.S.-British Nation Now Could Break Fascism; Lay Basis for
   Union of Free Peoples."
New Leader, July 13, 1940, p. 5.

B397 "Only U.S. War on German Axis Can Stop World Totalitarianism."
New Leader, August 31, 1940, p. 3.

B398 "The Passive Barbarian."
Atlantic Monthly, CLXVI (September 1940), 274–76.

Taken from Mumford's *Faith for Living* (1940), where it appears as Chapter 7 with the title "The Primitive and the Personal."

B399 "The Sky Line: The Brooklyn Library."
New Yorker, XVI (October 19, 1940), 47–48.

B400 "How They Are Voting."
New Republic, CIII (October 21, 1940), 554.

A short paragraph by Mumford replying to the editors' request for his presidential preference.

B401 "The Sky Line: Skyscraper School."
New Yorker, XVI (November 16, 1940), 71–72.

B402 "The Sky Line: Cloud over Sixth Avenue; Home on the Park."
New Yorker, XVI (December 21, 1940), 78–80.

1941

B403 "This Challenge to World Democracy."
Federal Union World, III (January 1941), 1+.

B404 "The Sky Line: New Terminal; New School."
New Yorker, XVII (March 8, 1941), 66–68.

B405 "Demand for Peace Terms Is Maneuver to Break Britain."
New Leader, March 15, 1941, p. 7.

B406 "World Reorganization Possible If Germany Aids in Rooting out Its Power Instincts."
New Leader, March 22, 1941, p. 4.

B407 "The Aftermath of Utopianism."
Christianity and Crisis, I (March 24, 1941), 2–7.

Included in the collection of Mumford's essays, *Values for Survival* (1946).

B408 "The State of the Union—Mumford."
Columbia Sentinel (Columbia University), April 3, 1941, p. 1+.

B409 "The Sky Line: The Architecture of Power."
New Yorker, XVII (June 7, 1941), 58–60.

B410 "Lewis Mumford Urges: United States Attack Axis Armies Now."
New Leader, June 7, 1941, p. 5.

B411 "California's Possibilities; Aims for the Post-War World; The City of the Future; Planning in a Democracy."
Agenda for Western Housing and Planning, I (July 1941), 3.

An interview with Mumford by the editor.

B412 "The Sky Line: Looking Forward, Looking Backward."
New Yorker, XVII (September 6, 1941), 47–49.

B413 "The Sky Line: Straightjackets and Zigzags."
New Yorker, XVII (October 18, 1941), 72–75.

B414 "The Sky Line: Outdoors and In."
New Yorker, XVII (December 6, 1941), 129–31.

B415 "Mumford Calls for Housecleaning in State Dept., Ouster of Hull, 'Routinized' Military, Navy Chiefs."
New Leader, December 13, 1941, p. 5.

1942

B416 "Urban Planning for War and Peace; An Address."
Fairmount Park Art Association (Philadelphia). *Seventieth Annual Report* (1942), p. 23+.

B417 "The Sky Line: Dynamics and Domesticity."
New Yorker, XVII (January 3, 1942), 52–54.

B418 "Leisure to Replace Work."
Science Digest, XI (February 1942), 5–8.

Taken from a chapter in Mumford's *Technics and Civilization* (1934).

B419 "The Sky Line: Closed-In Parks and Open Shops."
New Yorker, XVII (February 7, 1942), 52–54.

B420 "Save the Seed Corn."
New Republic, CVI (February 16, 1942), 227–29.

B421 "The Sky Line: Making Taxpayers Pay Taxes."
New Yorker, XVIII (March 14, 1942), 42+.

B422 "The Sky Line: New Era."
New Yorker, XVIII (April 25, 1942), 61–64.

B423 "The Sky Line: War and Peace."
New Yorker, XVIII (May 23, 1942), 56–58.

B424 "A Long-Term View of the War."
Progressive Education, XIX (November 1942), 358–60.

A talk presented to students and faculty at Stanford University on October 6, 1942.

1943

B425 "The Taste of New England."
New Yorker, XIX (February 27, 1943), 20.

A poem taken from Mumford's unfinished novel in verse, *Victor*.

Included in the collection of Mumford's essays and other writings, *The Human Prospect* (1955).

B426 "Whose 'Unconditional Surrender'?"
New Leader, August 14, 1943, p. 5.

1944

B427 "Hast Thou Conquered, Galilean? A Modern View of Jesus of Nazareth."
Menorah Journal, XXXII (Spring: April–June 1944), 61–74.

A slightly revised chapter taken from Mumford's *The Condition of Man* (1944).

B428 "Baldwin Hills Village."
Pencil Points, XXV (September 1944), 44–45.

B429 "Advice to Those in Danger."
Saturday Review of Literature, XXVII (October 21, 1944), 25.

A poem.

B430 "Justice to the Victims of Fascism."
New Leader, October 28, 1944, p. 6.

B431 "Consolation in War."
New Yorker, XX (November 25, 1944), 27.

A poem.

Included, with the title "Consolation in Time of War," in the collection of Mumford's essays and other writings, *The Human Prospect* (1955). Also in *'New Yorker' Book of Poems*. New York: Viking Press, 1969.

1945

B432 "Lewis Mumford on the Future of London."
Architectural Review, XCVII (January 1945), 3-10.

B433 "Monuments and Memorials."
Good Housekeeping, CXX (January 1945), 17+.

B434 "American Introduction to Sir Ebenezer Howard's *Garden Cities of Tomorrow*."
Pencil Points, XXVI (March 1945), 73-78.

B435 "At Parting."
Saturday Review of Literature, XXVIII (March 10, 1945), 18.

A poem.

B436 "From Two Letters Written after the Death of His Son Who Was Killed in Action."
Twice A Year, XII-XIII—Double number (Spring–Summer, Fall–Winter 1945), 16.

B437 "Admonition to Those Bereaved in War."
Twice A Year, XII-XIII—Double number (Spring–Summer, Fall–Winter 1945), 353-56.

A poem.

B438 "A Letter to a German Writer."
Saturday Review of Literature, XXVIII (December 8, 1945), 7-9+.

Included in slightly longer version in the collection of Mumford's essays, *Values for Survival* (1946), with the title "To Alfons F., A German Writer in Austria."

1946

B439 "The Manchester Plan."
Manchester Guardian (newspaper), January 12, 1946, p. 4+.

B440 "A Letter to a German Professor."
Saturday Review of Literature, XXIX (January 19, 1946), 5–6+.

Included, slightly expanded, in the collection of Mumford's essays, *Values for Survival* (1946), with the title "To E.A.T., A Professor of Philosophy in Munich."

B441 "Garden Cities and the Metropolis: A Reply."
Journal of Land and Public Utility Economics, XXII (February 1946), 66–69.

B442 "Gentlemen: You Are Mad!"
Saturday Review of Literature, XXIX (March 2, 1946), 5–6.

B443 "Members One of Another."
City College Alumnus (N.Y.), XLII (May 1946), 61–62+.

An address in remembrance of the alumni and students who gave their lives in World War II, delivered in the Great Hall on Charter Day, May 7, 1946.

B444 [Remarks at the Presentation of] "the Howard Memorial Medal."
Builder, July 12, 1946, pp. 43–44.

Mumford's remarks, in part, upon being presented the Medal by the President of the Town and Country Planning Association.

B445 "Human Problems of Dispersal."
Town and Country Planning, XIV (Summer 1946), 70–73.

Welwyn Lecture delivered at Welwyn Garden City, England. "Points from this talk are printed here." Editor's note.

B446 "Address by Mr. Lewis Mumford" [at the Annual General Meeting of the Town Planning Institute. With Discussion.]
Town Planning Institute. Journal, XXXII (July/August 1946), 175–80.

Also published, with minor changes and slightly shortened, in *Architect and Building News*, CLXXXVI (June 28, 1946), 203–05.

Address also published, without the discussion and slightly shortened, in *Architects' Journal*, CIV (July 4, 1946), 18–19.

B447 "A World Centre for the United Nations."
Royal Institute of British Architects. Journal, series 3, LIII (August 1946), 427–34.

A lecture, including questions from the floor, presented to the Royal Institute of British Architects, July 12, 1946.

A briefer and somewhat altered version of this lecture was published with the same title in *Progressive Architecture-Pencil Points*, XXVII (August 1946), 70–72.

B448 "The British Character as I See It."
Listener, XXXVI (August 8, 1946), 167–68.

B449 "Britain and Her Planning Schemes."
Listener, XXXVI (August 15, 1946), 201–02.

Reprinted in *Parents' Review*, LVII (October 1946), 215–18.

1947
B450 "The Nature of Our Age."
Sociological Review, XXXIX (Section one, 1947), 82–84.

Summary of a lecture prepared from notes by Miss E. D. Aitken and later corrected by Mumford. Lecture given at the annual conference of the Institute of Sociology (Le Play House) held at Reading University in England, July 26 to August 2, 1946.

B451 "Atom Bomb: Social Effects."
Air Affairs, I (March 1947), 370–82.

Included in the collection of Mumford's essays, *In the Name of Sanity* (1954), with the title "Assumptions and Predictions."

B452 "Transfiguration or Renewal?"
Pacific Spectator, I (August 1947), 391–98.

B453 "The Sky Line: Status Quo."
New Yorker, XXIII (October 11, 1947), 104–06.

B454 "The Sky Line: United Nations Headquarters: The Ground Plan."
New Yorker, XXIII (October 25, 1947), 56+.

Included in the collection of Mumford's essays, *From the Ground Up* (1956), with the title "UN Model and Model UN."

B455 "What Should Our Cities Be Like?"
Architectural League of New York, 1947. 5 pages (mimeographed).

A summary of a discussion at the Architectural League of New York, October 16, 1947.

B456   "The Sky Line: United Nations Headquarters: Buildings as
        Symbols."
        New Yorker, XXIII (November 15, 1947), 102+.

        Included in the collection of Mumford's essays, *From the Ground
        Up* (1956), with the title "Buildings as Symbols."

B457   "The Rights of Man."
        United Nations Bulletin, III (November 25, 1947), 694.

B458   "The Sky Line: The Best Is Yet to Come."
        New Yorker, XXIII (December 13, 1947), 85–86+.

1948

B459   "The Nature of Fascism."
        Dartmouth Alumni Magazine, XL (January 1948), 11–15.

        Lecture given in the Great Issues Course, November 6, 1947.

B460   "The Sky Line: Outside Looking In."
        New Yorker, XXIII (February 14, 1948), 58+.

B461   "What Is Happening to Modern Architecture? A Symposium at
        the Museum of Modern Art."
        New York Museum of Modern Art. Bulletin, XV (Spring 1948),
        18–19.

B462   "The Sky Line: Manhattan, Inside and Out."
        New Yorker, XXIV (May 15, 1948), 80+.

B463   "Cities Fit to Live In."
        Nation, CLXVI (May 15, 1948), 530–33.

        Reprinted in *One Hundred Years of 'The Nation.'* Edited by H. M.
        Christman. New York: Macmillan Co., 1965.

B464   "Kindling for Global Gehenna."
        Saturday Review of Literature, XXXI (June 26, 1948), 7–8+.

B465   "Atom Bomb: 'Miracle' or Catastrophe?"
        Air Affairs, II (July 1948), 326–45.

        Included in the collection of Mumford's essays, *In the Name of
        Sanity* (1954), with the title " 'Miracle' or Catastrophe."

        Reprinted and published as a pamphlet with the title *Atomic War—
        the Way Out*. Peace Aims Pamphlet 46. London: National Peace
        Council, [1948?]. 19p.

B466 "Let Man Take Command."
Saturday Review of Literature, XXXI (October 2, 1948), 7–9+.

Based on an address given at the centenary meeting of the American Association for the Advancement of Science held in Washington, D.C., September 13–17, 1948.

Reprinted in slightly longer form in *Perspectives*, no. 11 (Spring 1955), 77–94, with the title "Technics and the Future of Western Civilization."

Included with the latter title in the collection of Mumford's essays, *In the Name of Sanity* (1954).

B467 "The Sky Line: Prefabricated Blight."
New Yorker, XXIV (October 30, 1948), 49–50+.

Included in the collection of Mumford's essays, *From the Ground Up* (1956).

B468 "The Sky Line: Stuyvesant Town Revisited."
New Yorker, XXIV (November 27, 1948), 65–72.

B469 "The Sky Line: New Faces."
New Yorker, XXIV (December 4, 1948), 100+.

B470 "The Goals of Planning."
American Society of Planning Officials. *Planning 1948*. Proceedings of the annual National Planning Conference of the American Society of Planning Officials held in New York City, October 11–13, 1948, pp. 1–7.

Major portions of this article reprinted in *Journal of Housing*, VI (January 1949), 7–10, with the title "The 'Good Life' Must Be a Goal of City Planning."

1949

B471 "The Sky Line: The Quick and the Dead."
New Yorker, XXIV (January 8, 1949), 60+.

B472 "The Sky Line: Business, But Not As Usual."
New Yorker, XXV (February 26, 1949), 61–65.

B473 "Monumentalism, Symbolism and Style."
Architectural Review, CV (April 1949), 173–80.

Reprinted in *Magazine of Art*, XLII (October 1949), 202–07+; (November 1949), 258–63.

Included in the collection of Mumford's essays and other writings, *The Human Prospect* (1955).

B474 "Planning for the Phases of Life."
Town Planning Review, XX (April 1949), 5–16.

Included in Mumford's collection of essays, *The Urban Prospect* (1968).

B475 "A Thought for a Growing South."
Southern Packet, V (April 1949), 1–5.

B476 "The Sky Line: Accent on Openings."
New Yorker, XXV (April 16, 1949), 62 +.

B477 "The Sky Line: Design for Living."
New Yorker, XXV (June 25, 1949), 72–76.

B478 "The Sky Line: The Genteel and the Genuine."
New Yorker, XXV (July 9, 1949), 42–46.

B479 "The Fallacy of Systems."
Saturday Review of Literature, XXXII (October 1, 1949), 8–9.

This article, with some minor changes and some additional material, is part of a chapter in Mumford's *The Conduct of Life* (1951).

B480 "The Sky Line: From Utopia Parkway Turn East."
New Yorker, XXV (October 22, 1949), 102–06.

Included in Mumford's *From the Ground Up* (1956).

B481 "The Sky Line: The Great Good Place."
New Yorker, XXV (November 12, 1949), 73–78.

Included in Mumford's *From the Ground Up* (1956), with the title "Fresh Meadows, Fresh Plans."

1950

B482 "Laertes' Weapon."
Common Cause, III (January 1950), 281–83.

B483 "Mirror of a Violent Half Century."
New York Times Book Review, January 15, 1950, p. 1 +.

Included with the title "Mirrors of Violence" in the collection of Mumford's essays, *In the Name of Sanity* (1954).

B484 "The Sky Line: Civic Virtue."
New Yorker, XXV (February 4, 1950), 58–63.

B485 "The Sky Line: The Plight of the Prosperous."
New Yorker, XXVI (March 4, 1950), 68+.

Included in the collection of Mumford's essays, *From the Ground Up* (1956).

B486 "The Sky Line: The Mud Wasps of Manhattan."
New Yorker, XXVI (March 25, 1950), 64+.

B487 "Alternatives to Catastrophe."
Air Affairs, III (Spring 1950), 350–63.

B488 "The Sky Line: The Red-Brick Beehives."
New Yorker, XXVI (May 6, 1950), 92+.

B489 "The Sky Line: The Gentle Art of Overcrowding."
New Yorker, XXVI (May 20, 1950), 79–83.

Included in the collection of Mumford's essays, *From the Ground Up* (1956).

B490 "The Sky Line: Bigger Slums or Better City?"
New Yorker, XXVI (June 24, 1950), 78–84.

B491 "Regional Planning and the Small Town."
American Institute of Architects. Journal, new series, XIV (July 1950), 3–10; (August 1950), 82–91.

An address delivered to the American Institute of Architects' Convention Symposium I, "Urban and Regional Planning," in Washington, D.C., May 13, 1950.

B492 "Mumford on Geddes."
Architectural Review, CVIII (August 1950), 81–87.

Reprinted in slightly altered form in *Magazine of Art*, XLIV (January 1951), 25–31, with the title "Patrick Geddes and His *Cities in Evolution*."

Included in the collection of Mumford's essays and other writings, *The Human Prospect* (1955), with the title "Patrick Geddes," but lacking the short final section entitled "Postscript on Geddes' Writings."

B493 "The Sky Line: In Memoriam."
New Yorker, XXVI (November 18, 1950), 87–90+.

B494 "Frederick Lee Ackerman, F.A.I.A., 1878–1950."
American Institute of Architects. Journal, new series, XIV (December 1950), 249–54.

1951

B495 "The Salvation of Letters."
Academy Papers; Addresses on the Evangeline Wilbour Blashfield Foundation of the American Academy of Arts and Letters. New York: [American Academy of Arts and Letters], 1951, pp. 158–73.

This address was presented in 1942 at the National Institute of Arts and Letters.

B496 "Man as Interpreter."
Pacific Spectator, V (no. 2, 1951), 196–205.

Preprint of a chapter in Mumford's *The Conduct of Life* (1951).

B497 "In the Name of Sanity."
Common Cause, IV (February 1951), 337–40.

Included with alterations and somewhat shortened as the title essay in the collection of Mumford's essays, *In the Name of Sanity* (1954).

B498 "The Sky Line: More Pelion, More Ossa."
New Yorker, XXVI (February 3, 1951), 76+.

B499 "The Sky Line: Masterpiece of Mediocrity."
New Yorker, XXVII (March 10, 1951), 85–89.

B500 "The Sky Line: Artful Blight."
New Yorker, XXVII (May 5, 1951), 84–90.

B501 "The Sky Line: Magic with Mirrors—I."
New Yorker, XXVII (September 15, 1951), 84+.

Included in the collection of Mumford's essays, *From the Ground Up* (1956).

B502 "The Sky Line: Magic with Mirrors—II."
New Yorker, XXVII (September 22, 1951), 99–100+.

Included in Mumford's *From the Ground Up* (1956), with the title "A Disoriented Symbol."

B503 "Function and Expression in Architecture."
Architectural Record, CX (November 1951), 106–12.

B504 "The Sky Line: High, White, and Handsome."
New Yorker, XXVII (November 17, 1951), 165–71.

B505 "Matthew Nowicki."
North Carolina State College, School of Design. Student Publication, no. 1 (Winter 1951), 7.

An excerpt from Mumford's statement that accompanied an exhibition of sketches and photographs of Nowicki's architectural projects displayed at the Museum of Modern Art, New York City, in September 1950. The complete text of this statement has not been published.

A briefer and somewhat different excerpt was published in *Architectural Forum*, XCIII (October 1950), 201.

B506 "The Sky Line: Big Buildings and Tremendous Trifles."
New Yorker, XXVII (December 22, 1951), 60–65.

1952

B507 "Standardization, Reproduction and Choice."
Magazine of Art, XLV (February 1952), 51–57.

Condensed from one of six Bampton Lectures delivered at Columbia University in Spring 1951. The Lectures were published in Mumford's *Art and Technics* (1952).

B508 "The Sky Line: Fresh Start."
New Yorker, XXVIII (March 8, 1952), 72–78.

Included in the collection of Mumford's essays, *From the Ground Up* (1956).

B509 "The Sky Line: Schools for Human Beings—I."
New Yorker, XXVIII (April 19, 1952), 65–66+.

Included in Mumford's *From the Ground Up* (1956).

B510 "The Sky Line: Schools for Human Beings—II."
New Yorker, XXVIII (April 26, 1952), 68–74.

B511 "The Tyranny of Technics."
Commonweal, LVI (May 16, 1952), 135–37.

This article is a section of Mumford's book, *Art and Technics* (1952).

B512 "The Sky Line: House of Glass."
New Yorker, XXVIII (August 9, 1952), 48–54.

Included in Mumford's *From the Ground Up* (1956).

B513 "The Sky Line: Fifth Avenue, for Better or Worse."
New Yorker, XXVIII (August 16, 1952), 51–54+.

B514 "Where Did the Contemporary American House Come from?"
House Beautiful, XCIV (October 1952), 200–01+.

An excerpt from Mumford's essay, "A Backward Glance," published in *Roots of Contemporary American Architecture* (1952).

B515 "The Sky Line: Preview of the Past."
New Yorker, XXVIII (October 11, 1952), 66+.

B516 "Rebirth of the Family."
House Beautiful, XCIV (December 1952), 118–21+.

Derived from Mumford's book, *Faith for Living* (1940); not a reprint of Chapter 34 with the same title.

1953

B517 "What [Adlai] Stevenson Started."
New Republic, CXXVIII (January 5, 1953), 9–10.

B518 "The Sky Line: Workshop Invisible."
New Yorker, XXVIII (January 17, 1953), 83–88.

Included in the collection of Mumford's essays, *From the Ground Up* (1956).

B519 "Architecture: Beautiful and Beloved."
New York Times Magazine, part 2, February 1, 1953, pp. 22–23.

B520 "Education for Today's World."
Simmons College Bulletin, February 1953, pp. 16–17.

Address given at Simmons' Mid-century Jubilee Conference.

B521 "The Sky Line: United Nations Assembly."
New Yorker, XXIX (March 14, 1953), 72+.

Reprinted in *Royal Architectural Institute of Canada. Journal*, XXX (April 1953), 108–10, with the title "General Assembly Building."

Included in the collection of Mumford's essays, *From the Ground Up* (1956).

B522 "Philadelphia, Present, Probable and Possible."
Fairmount Park Art Association (Philadelphia). *Proceedings of the Eighty-First Annual Meeting*, 1953, pp. 15–29.

B523 "The Sky Line: From Blight to Beauty—I."
New Yorker, XXIX (April 25, 1953), 102–07.

Included in the collection of Mumford's essays, *From the Ground Up* (1956), with the title "Municipal Functions and Civic Art."

B524 "The Sky Line: From Blight to Beauty—II."
New Yorker, XXIX (May 9, 1953), 91–97.

Included in Mumford's *From the Ground Up* (1956), with the title "Closed Minds and Open Spaces."

B525 "The House with an Interior."
House Beautiful, XCV (June 1953), 128–30+.

B526 "The High-Rise Fashion."
Town and Country Planning, XXI (July 1953), 312–18.

An address delivered at the annual general meeting of the Town and Country Planning Association, May 13, 1953.

B527 "Talk by Mr. Lewis Mumford Given at the A.A. (Architectural Association) on May 26, 1953."
Architectural Association Journal, LXIX (July/August 1953), 48–51.

Also published in *Royal Architectural Institute of Canada. Journal*, XXX (September 1953), 268–71; and in *Architects' Journal*, CXVIII (July 9, 1953), 56–58.
The article in *Architects' Journal* does not include the full text of the question-and-answer period, but it does contain photographs that do not appear in the other two journals cited.

B528 "A Successful Demonstration."
Town and Country Planning, XXI (September 1953), 413–14.

Based on passages in Mumford's *The Culture of Cities* (1938).

B529 "The Sky Line: The Liveliness of London."
New Yorker, XXIX (September 19, 1953), 98–103.

B530 "The Sky Line: East End Urbanity."
New Yorker, XXIX (September 26, 1953), 100+.

Included in the collection of Mumford's essays, *The Highway and the City* (1963).

B531 "The Sky Line: Old Forms for New Towns."
New Yorker, XXIX (October 17, 1953), 138–46.

Included in Mumford's *The Highway and the City* (1963).

B532 "The Sky Line: A Phoenix Too Infrequent—I."
New Yorker, XXIX (November 28, 1953), 133–39.

Included in Mumford's *From the Ground Up* (1956), with the title "The Fujiyama of Architecture."

B533 "The Sky Line: A Phoenix Too Infrequent—II."
New Yorker, XXIX (December 12, 1953), 116–20+.

Included in Mumford's *From the Ground Up* (1956).

1954

B534 "The America in Europe."
Comprendre (Société Européene de Culture), nos. 10–11 (May 1954), 161–64.

Included in the collection of Mumford's essays and other writings, *The Human Prospect* (1955).

B535 "Anticipations and Social Consequences of Atomic Energy."
American Philosophical Society. *Proceedings* (1954), XCVIII (no. 2), 149–52.

Originally delivered as an address to the American Philosophical Society in Philadelphia in November 1953.

Also published in *Bulletin of the Atomic Scientists*, X (February 1954), 34–36. Mumford replies to comment on this article in the same volume, issue of May 1954, pages 159–60.

B536 "The Neighborhood and the Neighborhood Unit."
Town Planning Review, XXIV (January 1954), 256–70.

Included in the collection of Mumford's essays, *The Urban Prospect* (1968).

B537 "The Sky Line: Terminals and Monuments."
New Yorker, XXX (March 20, 1954), 101–02+.

B538 "Irrational Elements in Art and Politics."
New Republic, CXXX (April 5, 1954), 16–18; (April 12, 1954), 17–19.

A talk given at the Corcoran Gallery in Washington, D.C., in January 1954, under the auspices of the Institute of Contemporary Arts and the Phillips Gallery.

Included in the collection of Mumford's essays, *In the Name of Sanity* (1954).

B539 "Alternatives to the H-Bomb."
New Leader, XXXVII (June 28, 1954), 4–9.

Part of this article originally appeared in *Air Affairs*, II (July 1948), 326–45, with the title "Atom Bomb: 'Miracle' or Catastrophe?"

This article included with the title "The Art of the 'Impossible,'" in

Alternatives to the H-Bomb by Lewis Mumford and others. Edited by Anatole Shub. Boston: Beacon Press, 1955.

B540 "The Life, the Teaching and the Architecture of Matthew Nowicki."
Architectural Record:

Part I: no subtitle.
CXV (June 1954), 139–49.

Part II: "Matthew Nowicki as an Educator."
CXVI (July 1954), 128–35.

Part III: "His Architectural Achievement."
CXVI (August 1954), 169–75.

Part IV: Nowicki's Work in India."
CXVI (September 1954), 153–59.

B541 "Alexander Farquharson: A Friend's Memories."
Sociological Review, new series, II (July 1954), 5–10.

B542 "The Philosophy of Storage."
House Beautiful, XCVI (August 1954), 58–59+.

B543 "The Civic Contributions of Patrick Geddes."
International Federation of Housing and Town Planning. News Sheet, no. 33 (August 1954), 5–8.

B544 "The Rise of Caliban."
Virginia Quarterly Review, XXX (Summer 1954), 321–41.

A lecture given at Brooklyn College in May 1954 under the sponsorship of the Franklin Matchette Foundation.

Included in the collection of Mumford's essays, *In the Name of Sanity* (1954), with the title "The Uprising of Caliban."

B545 "The Sky Line: Windows and Gardens."
New Yorker, XXX (October 2, 1954), 121–24+.

Included in Mumford's *From the Ground Up* (1956).

B546 "The Sky Line: Skin Treatment and New Wrinkles."
New Yorker, XXX (October 23, 1954), 132–38.

Included, somewhat shortened, in Mumford's *From the Ground Up* (1956).

B547 "The Sky Line: Crystal Lantern."
New Yorker, XXX (November 13, 1954), 197–204.

Included in Mumford's *From the Ground Up* (1956).

B548 "The Sky Line: Charivari and Confetti."
New Yorker, XXX (December 18, 1954), 114-19.

1955

B549 "Garden Civilizations: Preparing for a New Epoch."
Town and Country Planning, XXIII (March 1955), 138-42.

A previously unpublished essay, written in 1917, when Mumford was twenty-one.

B550 "Arts and the Man."
American Institute of Architects. Journal, new series, XXIII (March 1955), 99-103; (April 1955), 165-70.

An address to the Columbia University conference on "The Role of the University in the Creative Arts," November 13, 1954.

B551 "The Sky Line: The Roaring Traffic's Boom—I."
New Yorker, XXXI (March 19, 1955), 115-21.

Included in the collection of Mumford's essays, *From the Ground Up* (1956), with the title "Is New York Expendable?"

B552 "The Sky Line: The Roaring Traffic's Boom—II."
New Yorker, XXXI (April 2, 1955), 97-103.

Included in Mumford's *From the Ground Up* (1956), with the title "The Two-Way Flood."

B553 "The Sky Line: The Roaring Traffic's Boom—III."
New Yorker, XXXI (April 16, 1955), 78-79+.

Included in Mumford's *From the Ground Up* (1956), with the title "Restored Circulation, Renewed Life."

B554 "Whitman and the Democratic Idea: 'Justice Is Always in Jeopardy.'"
New Leader, XXXVIII (May 16, 1955), 16-18.

Mumford's address at the dedication of Whitman Auditorium, Brooklyn College.

B555 "The Sky Line: The Roaring Traffic's Boom—IV."
New Yorker, XXXI (June 11, 1955), 86-94+.

Included in Mumford's *From the Ground Up* (1956), with the title "From the Ground Up."

B556 "The Sky Line: Museum or Kaleidoscope?"
New Yorker, XXXI (October 15, 1955), 166+.

Included in Mumford's *From the Ground Up* (1956).

1956

B557 "The Sky Line: The Drab and the Daring."
New Yorker, XXXI (February 4, 1956), 82–88.

B558 "Opinions on the New Towns."
Town and Country Planning, XXIV (March 1956), 161–64.

B559 "The Sky Line: Philadelphia—I."
New Yorker, XXXII (April 28, 1956), 118+.

B560 "For Older People—Not Segregation but Integration."
Architectural Record, CXIX (May 1956), 191–94.

Included, with the title "Quarters for an Aging Population," in the collection of Mumford's essays, *The Urban Prospect* (1968).

B561 "A Study of History."
Diogenes; An International Review of Philosophy and Humanistic Studies, no. 13 (Spring 1956), 11–28.

B562 "The Sky Line: Philadelphia—II."
New Yorker, XXXII (May 26, 1956), 121–24+.

B563 "The Sky Line: The Gift Horse's Mouth."
New Yorker, XXXII (September 22, 1956), 137–43.

Reprinted in *Royal Architectural Institute of Canada. Journal*, XXXIV (May 1957), 181–83.

B564 "The Sky Line: Philadelphia—I."
New Yorker, XXXII (November 17, 1956), 138–40+.

This article and three subsequent ones cited below with the title "Historic Philadelphia" are included in the collection of Mumford's essays, *The Highway and the City* (1963).

1957

B565 "A New Approach to Workers' Housing."
International Labour Review, LXXV (February 1957), 93–103.

Also published in *Town and Country Planning*, XXV (April 1957), 151–61.

B566   "The Sky Line: Historic Philadelphia—II."
        New Yorker, XXXII (February 9, 1957), 100–06.

B567   "The Sky Line: Historic Philadelphia—III."
        New Yorker, XXXIII (April 6, 1957), 132–41.

B568   "The Sky Line: Historic Philadelphia—IV."
        New Yorker, XXXIII (April 13, 1957), 155–62.

B569   "Address: Summary and Outlook."
        Connecticut General Life Insurance Co. *The New Highways: Challenge to the Metropolitan Region*. A Symposium. Hartford, Connecticut, [1957], section Z 1792, pp. 1–14.

        Mumford's address at the Symposium on September 11, 1957. The substance of this address is contained in Mumford's essay "The Highway and the City" included in his collection of essays, *The Highway and the City* (1963).

B570   "The Sky Line: Babel in Europe."
        New Yorker, XXXIII (September 28, 1957), 124+.

        This article is included in Mumford's *The Highway and the City* (1963).

B571   "The Role of the Creative Arts in Contemporary Society."
        Virginia Quarterly Review, XXXIII (Fall 1957), 521–38.

        Presented as an address at the University of New Hampshire, February 28, 1957.

        Published separately with the same title: Durham, N.H.: University of New Hampshire, 1958. 23p.

B572   "The Sky Line: The Marseilles 'Folly.' "
        New Yorker, XXXIII (October 5, 1957), 76+.

        This article is included in the collection of Mumford's essays, *The Highway and the City* (1963).

B573   "The Sky Line: A Walk through Rotterdam."
        New Yorker, XXXIII (October 12, 1957), 174+.

        Included as a chapter in Mumford's *The Highway and the City* (1963).

        This article and the one of November 2, 1957, were reprinted, in large part, with photographs in *Delta, A Review of Arts, Life and Thought in the Netherlands*, I (Summer 1958), 3–17, with the title

"The Rebuilding of Rotterdam: The Mall, the Memorial, the Beehive, and the Flower."

B574 "The Sky Line: The Cave, the City, and the Flower."
New Yorker, XXXIII (November 2, 1957), 93–94+.

Included in the collection of Mumford's essays, *The Highway and the City* (1963).

See note added to *New Yorker* article of October 12, 1957.

1958

B575 "Boston's Backwardness Is Its Principal Asset."
Boston College. College of Business Administration. *Proceedings of the 1957–58 Series of Citizens Seminars on the Fiscal, Economical and Political Problems of Boston and the Metropolitan Community*, 1958, pp. 40–44.

An address.

B576 "The Highway and the City."
Architectural Record, CXXIII (April 1958), 179–86.

Included in two of the collections of Mumford's essays: *The Highway and the City* (1963) and *The Urban Prospect* (1968).

B577 "The Sky Line: The Disappearance of Pennsylvania Station."
New Yorker, XXXIV (June 7, 1958), 97–104.

With the title "The Pennsylvania Station Nightmare," this essay appears in Mumford's *The Highway and the City* (1963).

This article was reprinted under its original title in *American Institute of Architects. Journal*, new series, XXX (October 1958), 40–43.

B578 "Presentation" [of the Gold Medal for Architecture to Henry R. Shepley].
Boston Society of Architects. A Record of the Activities of the Society, XLIII (July 1958), 1.

Presentation made at the American Academy of Arts and Letters.

B579 "Traffic vs. a Balanced Environment."
Landscape Architecture, XLVIII (July 1958), 241.

A letter Mumford wrote to a group (not named) that was fighting a battle against highway encroachment.

B580 "The Sky Line: The Lesson of the Master."
New Yorker, XXXIV (September 13, 1958), 141–48+.

Reprinted with the title "The Lesson of the Master: The Seagram Building" in *American Institute of Architects. Journal*, new series, XXXI (January 1959), 19–23.

1959

B581 "The Human Prospect and Architecture."
Architectural Record, CXXV (April 1959), 175–77.

An address to architectural students in Rome.

B582 "How War Began."
Saturday Evening Post, CCXXXI (April 18, 1959), 24–25+.

Also published in *Adventures of the Mind*. Edited by Richard Truelson and John Kobler. New York: Alfred Knopf, 1959.

B583 "An Appraisal of Lewis Mumford's *Technics and Civilization* (1934)."
Daedalus, LXXXVIII (Summer 1959), 527–36.

A review by Mumford a quarter of a century later.

B584 "The Moral Challenge to Democracy."
Virginia Quarterly Review, XXXV (Fall 1959), 560–76.

Revision of an address given at Dartmouth College in November 1958.

B585 "The Morals of Extermination."
Atlantic Monthly, CCIV (October 1959), 38–44.

Also published in *Breakthrough to Peace*. Norfolk, Conn.: New Directions Paperback, 1962.

B586 "The Sky Line: The Skyway's the Limit."
New Yorker, XXXV (November 14, 1959), 181–82+.

Included in the collection of Mumford's essays, *The Highway and the City* (1963).

B587 "The Sky Line: What Wright Hath Wrought."
New Yorker, XXXV (December 5, 1959), 105–06+.

Included as one of the essays in Mumford's *The Highway and the City* (1963).

1960

B588 "Planning and Nuclear Warfare; the Non-Governmental Side."
American Institute of Planners. *Proceedings of the 1960 Annual Conference*, 1960, pp. 22–26.

B589 "Frank Lloyd Wright, 1869–1959."
American Academy of Arts and Letters and the National Institute
of Arts and Letters. *Proceedings,* 2d series, no. 10. New York:
American Academy of Arts and Letters, 1960, pp. 382–86.

Included in Mumford's collection of essays, *The Highway and the
City* (1963), with the title "Postscript: In Memoriam: 1869–1959."

B590 "The Sky Line: It's Quicker to Walk."
New Yorker, XXXVI (September 3, 1960), 95–98+.

B591 "The Sky Line: UNESCO House—I. Out, Damned Cliché!"
New Yorker, XXXVI (November 12, 1960), 113–14+.

Included in Mumford's collection of essays, *The Highway and the
City* (1963).

B592 "The Sky Line: UNESCO House—II. The Hidden Treasure."
New Yorker, XXXVI (November 19, 1960), 213–20.

Included in Mumford's *The Highway and the City* (1963).

1961

B593 "The Social Function of Open Spaces."
Landscape, X (Winter 1960–61), 1–6.

An address presented before the International Federation of Landscape Architects, 7th Annual Congress, held in Amsterdam, June
20–22, 1960.

This article, slightly longer and including photographs, originally
published in *Space for Living.* Edited by Sylvia Crowe. Amsterdam:
Djambatan, 1961.

Reprinted with minor changes and without photographs in *Land-
scaping,* VI (January 1961), 12–13+, with the title "Landscape
Architecture in Relation to Town Planning and Sociology."

Included in Mumford's *The Highway and the City* (1963), with the
title "Landscape and Townscape," and in Mumford's *The Urban
Prospect* (1968).

B594 "On Freedom, Freeways, and Flexibility: The Private
     Correspondence of Messrs. Wolfe and Mumford."
American Institute of Planners. Journal, XXVII (February 1961),
75–77.

B595 "Culture of the City."
American Institute of Architects. Journal, new series, XXXV (June
1961), 54–60.

Address given at the 1961 convention of the American Institute of Architects.

B596 "The City in History."
Horizon, III (July 1961), 32–65.

Excerpts from Mumford's *The City in History* (1961), including photographs and illustrations.

B597 "History: Neglected Clue to Technological Change."
Technology and Culture, II (Summer 1961), 230–36.

Presented as an address at a joint program of the Society for the History of Technology and the American Historical Association in New York City, December 28, 1960.

B598 "Address upon Presentation of the Royal Gold Medal for Architecture."
Royal Institute of British Architects. Journal, 3d series, LXVIII (August 1961), 407–10.

Mumford's address upon receiving the Royal Gold Medal for Architecture.

Reprinted in *Arts and Architecture*, LXXIX (January 1962), 20–21+.

B599 "The City as Both Heaven and Hell; A Conversation between Graeme Shankland and Lewis Mumford."
Listener, LXVI (September 28, 1961), 463–65+.

A broadcast on the British Broadcasting Corporation's Third Programme, September 16, 1961.

Reprinted with the title "Both Heaven and Hell. A Conversation between Graeme Shankland and Lewis Mumford" in *Town Planning Institute. Journal*, XLVII (November 1961), 277–81.

B600 "Science as Technology."
American Philosophical Society. *Proceedings*, CV (October 1961), 506–11.

An address delivered at the University of Pennsylvania in Philadelphia on January 24, 1961, to the "Conference on the Influence of Science upon Modern Culture," sponsored jointly by the American Philosophical Society and the University of Pennsylvania to commemorate the 400th anniversary of the birth of Francis Bacon.

Included with slight changes in Mumford's *The Myth of the Machine: II. The Pentagon of Power* (1970).

B601 "Discussion with Lewis Mumford."
Architectural Association Journal, LXXVII (November 1961), 91–101.

An informal dinner discussion at the Architectural Association, June 29, 1960.

B602 "The Sky Line: London and the Laocoön."
New Yorker, XXXVII (November 4, 1961), 193–94+.

Included in the collection of Mumford's essays, *The Highway and the City* (1963), with the title "London—to the Skies!"

B603 "The Human Way Out."
Royal Institute of British Architects. Journal, 3d series, LXVIII (December 1961), 548–49.

An address given on September 28, 1961, at the University of California, Berkeley.

1962

B604 "The Sky Line: From Crotchet Castle to Arthur's Seat."
New Yorker, XXXVII (January 13, 1962), 82+.

Included in the collection of Mumford's essays, *The Highway and the City* (1963).

B605 "The Sky Line: Lady Godiva's Town."
New Yorker, XXXVIII (March 10, 1962), 93–94+.

One of the essays included in Mumford's *The Highway and the City* (1963).

B606 "Apology to Henry Adams."
Virginia Quarterly Review, XXXVIII (Spring 1962), 196–217.

Adapted from a lecture given in the autumn of 1961 at the University of California, Berkeley.

B607 "The Case against 'Modern Architecture.' "
Architectural Record, CXXXI (April 1962), 155–62.

One of the essays included in Mumford's *The Highway and the City* (1963).

B608 "The Future of the City."
Architectural Record:

Part I: "The Disappearing City."
CXXXII (October 1962), 121–28.

Part II: "Yesterday's City of Tomorrow."
CXXXII (November 1962), 139–44.

Part III: "Megalopolis as Anti-City."
CXXXII (December 1962), 101–08.

Part IV: "Beginnings of Urban Integration."
CXXXIII (January 1963), 119–26.

Part V: "Social Complexity and Urban Design."
CXXXIII (February 1963), 119–26.

These five articles included in the collection of Mumford's essays, *The Urban Prospect* (1968).

B609 "The Sky Line: False Front or Cold-War Concept."
New Yorker, XXXVIII (October 20, 1962), 174+.

Appears with title "Frozen-Faced Embassy" in Mumford's collection of essays, *The Highway and the City* (1963).

B610 "The Sky Line: Mother Jacobs' Home Remedies."
New Yorker, XXXVIII (December 1, 1962), 148+.

Included in Mumford's *The Urban Prospect* (1968), with the title "Home Remedies for Urban Cancer."

1963

B611 "The Sky Line: Not Yet Too Late."
New Yorker, XXXIX (December 7, 1963), 143–44+.

1964

B612 "The Automation of Knowledge."
Current Issues in Higher Education, 1964. Proceedings of the Nineteenth Annual National Conference on Higher Education, Chicago, April 19–22, 1964, pp. 11–21.

Address delivered at the opening general session.

Reprinted with a few changes and omissions in *Vital Speeches*, XXX (May 1, 1964), 441–46, and in *AV Communication Review*, XII (Fall 1964), 261–76.

Included in part in Mumford's *The Myth of the Machine: II. The Pentagon of Power* (1970).

B613 "Authoritarian and Democratic Technics."
Technology and Culture, V (Winter 1964), 1–8.

Mumford's address at the Fund for the Republic Tenth Anniversary Convocation on "Challenge to Democracy in the Next Decade," delivered in New York City, January 21, 1963.

Included in the book *Challenges to Democracy: The Next Ten Years*. Edited by Edward Reed. New York: Frederick A. Praeger, 1963.

This article was published in abridged form in *New Republic*, CXLVIII (February 16, 1963), 12–15, with the title "Now Let Man Take Over," and in *Science Digest*, LIV (July 1963), 85–89, with the title "Are We Selling Our Souls for Progress?"

1965

B614 "A New Regional Plan to Arrest Megalopolis."
Architectural Record, CXXXVII (March 1965), 147–54.

Included in the collection of Mumford's essays, *The Urban Prospect* (1968), with the title "Megalopolitan Dissolution vs. Regional Integration."

B615 "Utopia, the City and the Machine."
Daedalus, XCIV (Spring 1965), 271–92.

Included in the book *Utopias and Utopian Thought*. Edited by Frank E. Manuel. Boston: Houghton Mifflin, 1966.

B616 "On Guard! The City Is in Danger!"
University, A Princeton Quarterly, no. 24 (Spring 1965), 10–13.

This article was adapted from a lecture given at Princeton in November 1964.

Reprinted with the title, "In Defense of the City," in *Metropolitan Politics*. Edited by Michael Danielson. Boston: Little, Brown and Co., 1966.

B617 "Man the Finder."
Technology and Culture, VI (Summer 1965), 375–81.

From Mumford's *The Myth of the Machine: I. Technics and Human Development* (1967).

B618 [Address to the Association of Student Chapters, American Institute of Architects.]
Association of Student Chapters, American Institute of Architects. *Proceedings of the Convention of the Association of Student Chapters*, 1965, pp. 50–65.

Available only in typed form; original copy in the library of the American Institute of Architects, Washington, D.C.

B619 "New World Promise."
American Institute of Architects. Journal, new series, XLIV (August 1965), 43–47.

First annual Purves Memorial Lecture delivered at the joint convention of the American Institute of Architects and the Pan American Congress of Architects held in Washington, D.C., June 14–18, 1965. Simultaneously translated into Spanish.

B620 "Technics and the Nature of Man."
Nature, CCVIII (December 4, 1965), 923–28.

An address delivered at the Smithsonian Bicentennial celebration in September 1965.

Included as the Prologue to Mumford's *The Myth of the Machine: I. Technics and Human Development* (1967).

Included in the collection of essays, *Knowledge among Men.* Edited by Paul H. Oehser. New York: Simon and Schuster, 1966.

Also published in *Technology and Culture,* VII (Summer 1966), 303–17.

1966

B621 "The Disciple's Rebellion; A Memoir of Patrick Geddes."
Encounter, XXVII (September 1966), 11–21.

A chapter from Mumford's unfinished autobiography.

B622 "The First Megamachine."
Diogenes; An International Review of Philosophy and Humanistic Studies, no. 55 (Fall 1966), 1–5.

A chapter from Mumford's *The Myth of the Machine: I. Technics and Human Development* (1967).

B623 "Speculations on Prehistory."
American Scholar, XXXVI (Winter 1966–67), 43–53.

From Mumford's *The Myth of the Machine: I. Technics and Human Development* (1967).

B624 "Address" [as President of the American Academy of Arts and Letters.]
American Academy of Arts and Letters and the National Institute

of Arts and Letters. *Proceedings*, 2d series, no. 16. New York: American Academy of Arts and Letters, 1966, pp. 9–15.

1967

B625 "City Philosopher."
Boston, LIX (November 1967), 36–37.

An interview.

1968

B626 "Architecture as a Home for Man."
Architectural Record, CXLIII (February 1968), 113–16.

Excerpts taken from a paper read by Mumford on the occasion of receiving an honorary degree of Doctor of Architecture at a special convocation at the University of Rome in 1967.

B627 "Survival of Plants and Man."
Garden Journal, XVIII (May/June 1968), 66–71.

An address delivered at the final session of a symposium entitled "Challenge for Survival 1968: Land, Air and Water for Man in Megalopolis," sponsored by the New York Botanical Garden and the Rockefeller University, April 25–26, 1968.

Included in the collection of essays, *Challenge for Survival; Land, Air, and Water for Man in Megalopolis*. Edited by Pierre Dansereau. New York: Columbia University Press, 1970.

Published, with some changes, as a part of Chapter 14, in Mumford's *The Myth of the Machine: II. The Pentagon of Power* (1970).

B628 "Reflections; European Diary."
New Yorker, XLIV (July 6, 1968), 30–36+.

B629 "Comments on the Place of the Automobile in Society."
Saturday Evening Post, CCXLI (October 5, 1968), 34–35.

1969

B630 "Have Courage."
American Heritage, XX (February 1969), 104–11.

An adaptation of the introduction to *Essays and Journals*. by Ralph Waldo Emerson. Selected, and with an introduction by Lewis Mumford. Garden City, N.Y.: Doubleday and Co., 1968.

B631 "Prize:—or Lunacy?"
      Newsweek, LXXIV (July 7, 1969), 61.

      Statement on the eve of the flight of Apollo 11.

B632 "No: 'A Symbolic Act of War . . .' "
      New York Times, July 21, 1969, p. 6.

      Mumford's reactions to man's landing on the moon.

      1970

B633 "The Cult of Anti-Life."
      Virginia Quarterly Review, XLVI (Spring 1970), 198–206.

      Taken from Mumford's *The Myth of the Machine: II. The Pentagon of Power* (1970).

B634 "Reflections: The Megamachine—I."
      New Yorker, XLVI (October 10, 1970), 50–52+.

      This is the first part of a four-part article. The other parts were published as follows:

      "Reflections: The Megamachine—II."
      New Yorker, XLVI (October 17, 1970), 48–50+.

      "Reflections: The Megamachine—III."
      New Yorker, XLVI (October 24, 1970), 55–58+.

      "Reflections: The Megamachine—IV."
      New Yorker, XLVI (October 31, 1970), 50–52+.

      These four articles were taken from Mumford's *The Myth of the Machine: II. The Pentagon of Power* (1970).

B635 "The Pentagon of Power."
      Horizon, XII (Autumn 1970), 5–20.

      Taken from Mumford's *The Myth of the Machine: II. The Pentagon of Power* (1970).

B636 "Bring Back the Railroads."
      New York Times, October 9, 1970, p. 37.

C. BOOK REVIEWS

1918

C1 *Alsace-Lorraine under German Rule.* by Charles D. Hazen. New York: Henry Holt & Co.
   Public, A Journal of Democracy, XXI (April 27, 1918), 545.

1919

C2 *America and Britain.* by Andrew C. McLaughlin. New York: E. P. Dutton & Co.
   Explaining the Britishers. by Frederick W. Wile. New York: George H. Doran Co.
   Shaking Hands with England. by Charles H. Towne. New York: George H. Doran Co.
   Dial, LXVI (March 22, 1919), 298–99.

C3 *The World War and Its Consequences.* by William H. Hobbs. New York: G. P. Putnam's Sons.
   Dial, LXVI (April 19, 1919), 406–07.

C4 *The Little Town.* by Harlan Paul Douglass. New York: Macmillan Co.
   Nation, CVIII (May 24, 1919), 841–42.

An unsigned review.

C5 *Clemenceau: The Man and His Time.* by H. M. Hyndman. New York: F. A. Stokes Co.
   Clemenceau: The Tiger of France. by Georges Lecomte. New York: D. Appleton & Co.
   Dial, LXVII (July 12, 1919), 21–22.

C6 *Authority in the Modern State.* by Harold J. Laski. New Haven: Yale University Press.
   The State and the Nation. by Edward Jenks. New York: E. P. Dutton & Co.
   Dial, LXVII (July 26, 1919), 59–61.

C7   *Bolshevism and the United States.* by Charles E. Russell. Indianapolis: Bobbs-Merrill Co.
     Russia in 1919. by Arthur Ransome. New York: B. W. Huebsch.
       Dial, LXVII (August 23, 1919), 152–54.

C8   *Canon Barnett: His Life, Work, and Friends.* 2 vols. by Henrietta O. Barnett. Boston: Houghton Mifflin.
       Dial, LXVII (November 29, 1919), 473–75.

1920

C9   *In the World War.* by Count Ottokar Czernin. New York: Harper & Bros.
       Freeman, I (July 21, 1920), 452–53.

C10 *The Joke about Housing.* by Charles Harris Whitaker. Boston: Marshall, Jones Co.
       Freeman, I (August 4, 1920), 501.

1921

C11 *Social Theory.* by G. D. H. Cole. London: Methuen & Co.
       Sociological Review, XIII (January 1921), 52–54.

C12 *A History of the Chartist Movement.* by Julius West. Boston: Houghton Mifflin.
       Freeman, III (March 16, 1921), 22.

C13 *Theodore Roosevelt and His Time: Shown in His Own Letters.* 2 vols. by Joseph Bucklin Bishop. New York: Charles Scribner's Sons.
       Freeman, III (April 6, 1921), 93–94.

C14 *The Bolshevik Adventure.* by John Pollock. New York: E. P. Dutton and Co.
     Bolshevism: Theory and Practice. by Bertrand Russell. New York: Harcourt, Brace and Co.
     The Groping Giant: Revolutionary Russia as Seen by an American Democrat. New Haven: Yale University Press.
     Russia in the Shadows. by H. G. Wells. New York: George H. Doran.
       Freeman, III (April 27, 1921), 165–66.

C15 *The Group Mind: A Sketch of the Principles of Collective Psychology, with Some Attempt to Apply Them to the Interpretation of National Life and Character.* by William McDougall. Cambridge: Cambridge University Press.
       Sociological Review, XIII (July 1921), 184–86.

C16   *Glimpses of Bengal.* Selected from the letters of Rabindranath Tagore, 1885 to 1895. by Rabindranath Tagore. New York: Macmillan Co.
The Wreck: A Hindu Romance. by Rabindranath Tagore. New York: Macmillan Co.
Freeman, IV (September 28, 1921), 67–68.

C17   *Mechanism, Life and Personality: An Explanation of the Mechanistic Theory of Life.* by J. S. Haldane. New York: E. P. Dutton and Co.
Freeman, IV (October 19, 1921), 141–42.

C18   *Civilization: Its Cause and Cure, and Other Essays.* by Edward Carpenter. New York: Charles Scribner's Sons.
Freeman, IV (November 9, 1921), 211–12.

C19   *A London Mosaic.* by W. L. George. New York: F. A. Stokes.
London of the Future. edited by Sir Aston Webb. New York: E. P. Dutton & Co.
New Republic, XXVIII (November 9, 1921), 328–29.

C20   *The Engineers and the Price System.* by Thorstein Veblen. New York: B. W. Huebsch.
Freeman, IV (November 23, 1921), 261–62.

C21   *Mr. Punch's History of Modern England.* Vols. I–II. 1841–1874. by Charles L. Graves. New York: F. A. Stokes.
New Republic, XXIX (December 7, 1921), 50, 52.

Vols. III–IV reviewed in 1922.

1922

C22   *The Evolution of World Peace.* edited by F. S. Marvin. New York: Oxford University Press.
New Republic, XXIX (January 11, 1922), 187–88.

C23   *The Story of Mankind.* by Hendrik Willem Van Loon. New York: Boni and Liveright.
Freeman, IV (January 18, 1922), 449–50.

C24   *The Age of Invention.* by Holland Thompson. Vol. 37, *Chronicles of America.* New Haven: Yale University Press.
The Control of Life. by J. Arthur Thomson. New York: Henry Holt & Co.
New Republic, XXIX (February 15, 1922), 346, 348.

C25 *The Book of Jack London.* 2 vols. by Charmian London. New York: Century Co.
　　 New Republic, XXX (March 29, 1922), 145–47.

C26 *Rahab.* by Waldo Frank. New York: Boni and Liveright.
　　 New Republic, XXXI (August 16, 1922), 339–40.

C27 *Mr. Punch's History of Modern England.* Vols. III–IV. 1874–1914. by Charles L. Graves. New York: F. A. Stokes.
　　 New Republic, XXXII (September 20, 1922), 102–03.

　　 Vols. I–II reviewed in 1921.

C28 *Little Essays of Love and Virtue.* by Havelock Ellis. New York: George H. Doran Co.
　　 Sex and Common Sense. by A. Maude Royden. New York: G. P. Putnam's Sons.
　　 Freeman, VI (November 8, 1922), 213–14.

C29 *History of Art.* Vol. I: *Ancient Art.* Vol. II: *Medieval Art.* by Elie Faure. Translated by Walter Pach. New York: Harper & Bros.
　　 New Republic, XXXIII (November 29, 1922), part II, 1–2.

　　 Vols. III–IV reviewed in 1924.

1923

C30 *Anne Severn and the Fieldings.* by May Sinclair. New York: Macmillan Co.
　　 Nation, CXVI (January 24, 1923), 99.

C31 *Ariel.* by José Enrique Rodó. Translated with an introduction by F. J. Stimson. Boston: Houghton Mifflin.
　　 New Republic, XXXIII (February 7, 1923), 299–300.

C32 *David Lubin: A Study in Practical Idealism.* by Olivia Rossetti Agresti. Boston: Little, Brown and Co.
　　 Freeman, VI (February 21, 1923), 570–72.

C33 *Domestic Architecture of the American Colonies and of the Early Republic.* by Fiske Kimball. New York: Charles Scribner's Sons.
　　 New Republic, XXXIV (March 7, 1923), 48–50.

C34 *Paint.* by Thomas Craven. New York: Harcourt, Brace and Co.
　　 New Republic, XXXIV (April 4, 1923), 169–70.

C35 *The Significance of the Fine Arts.* by American Institute of Architects. Committee on Education. Boston: Marshall Jones & Co.
　　 New Republic, XXXIV (April 11, 1923), part II, 14+.

C36 *Waldo Frank; A Study.* by Gorham B. Munson. New York: Boni and Liveright.
 New Republic, XXXIV (May 2, 1923), 276.

C37 *Rossetti and His Circle.* by Max Beerbohm. Garden City, New York: Doubleday, Page and Co.
 Freeman, VII (May 9, 1923), 211–12.

C38 *The Interpreters.* by "A.E." New York: Macmillan Co.
 Freeman, VII (May 16, 1923), 235–37.

C39 *The Life of Reason: or the Phases of Human Progress.* 5 vols. by George Santayana. New York: Charles Scribner's Sons.
 Freeman, VII (May 23, 1923), 258–60.

C40 *The American Rhythm.* by Mary Austin. New York: Harcourt, Brace and Co.
 New Republic, XXXV (May 30, 1923), 23–24.

C41 *Three Plays.* by Luigi Pirandello. New York: E. P. Dutton and Co.
 Freeman, VII (June 13, 1923), 334.
 Signed L.C.M.

C42 *Men Like Gods: A Novel.* by H. G. Wells. New York: Macmillan Co.
 New Republic, XXXV (June 20, 1923), 102–03.

C43 *The History of Utopian Thought.* by Joyce O. Hertzler. New York: Macmillan Co.
 Literary Review, IV (June 23, 1923), 784.

C44 *Vincent van Gogh.* 2 vols. by Julius Meier-Graefe. Translated by John Holroyd Reece. Boston: The Medici Society.
 New Republic, XXXV (August 8, 1923), 296–97.

C45 *The Future of Painting.* by Willard Huntington Wright. New York: B. W. Huebsch.
 New Republic, XXXVI (September 12, 1923), 79–80.

C46 *The Architecture of Robert and James Adam (1758–1794).* 2 vols. by Arthur T. Bolton. New York: Charles Scribner's Sons.
 New Republic, XXXVI (October 3, 1923), 158.

C47 *The English Village: The Origin and Decay of Its Community; An Anthropological Interpretation.* by Harold Peake. London: Benn Brothers.
 American Institute of Architects. Journal, XI (October 1923), 414–16.

C48   *The Maritime History of Massachusetts: 1783–1860.* by Samuel Eliot Morison. Boston: Houghton Mifflin.
American Institute of Architects. Journal, XI (November 1923), 420–21.

C49   *Fancies Versus Fads.* by G. K. Chesterton. New York: Dodd, Mead and Co.
New Republic, XXXVII (December 26, 1923), 129.

1924

C50   *Housing Progress in Europe.* by Edith Elmer Wood. New York: E. P. Dutton and Co.
American Institute of Architects. Journal, XII (February 1924), 85–86.

C51   *Living Art, Twenty Facsimile Reproductions after Paintings, Drawings, and Engravings, and Ten Photographs after Sculpture by Contemporary Artists.* New York: Dial Publising Co.
New Republic, XXXVII (February 6, 1924), 290–91.

C52   *Early Connecticut Architecture.* by J. Frederick Kelly. New York: William Helburn, Inc.
American Institute of Architects. Journal, XII (May 1924), 251.

C53   *Ramsay MacDonald: The Man of Tomorrow.* by Iconoclast. Introduction by Oswald Garrison Villard. New York: Thomas Seltzer.
New Republic, XXXVIII (May 14, 1924), 316.

C54   *Town Planning and Town Development.* by S. D. Adshead. New York: E. P. Dutton and Co.
New Republic, XXXIX (June 11, 1924), 79–80.

C55   *The Autobiography of an Idea.* by Louis H. Sullivan. New York: Press of the American Institute of Architects.
New Republic, XXXIX (June 25, 1924), 132–33.

C56   *A Primer of Modern Art.* by Sheldon Cheney. New York: Boni and Liveright.
Western Art and the New Era: An Introduction to Modern Art. by Katherine S. Dreier. New York: Brentano's.
New Republic, XXXIX (July 9, 1924), 188–89.

C57   *My University Days.* by Maxim Gorky. New York: Boni and Liveright.
New Republic, XXXIX (July 23, 1924), 252.

C58 *History of Art*. Vol. III: *Renaissance Art*. Vol. IV: *Modern Art*. by Elie Faure. Translated by Walter Pach. New York: Harper & Bros.
New Republic, XXXIX (August 13, 1924), 335.

Vols. I–II reviewed in 1922.

C59 *Living Painters: Duncan Grant*. With an introduction by Roger Fry. London: The Hogarth Press.
The Necessity of Art. by A. Clutton Brock, et al. New York: G. H. Doran Co.
The Outline of Art. edited by Sir William Orpen. New York: G. P. Putnam's Sons.
Southern Baroque Art: A Study of Painting, Architecture and Music in Italy and Spain in the 17th and 18th Centuries. by Sacheverell Sitwell. New York: Alfred A. Knopf.
New Republic, XL (August 27, 1924), 397.

C60 *My Life in Art*. by Constantin Stanislavsky. Boston: Little, Brown & Co.
Saturday Review of Literature, I (September 6, 1924), 92.

C61 *Arnold Waterlow. A Life*. by May Sinclair. New York: Macmillan Co.
New York Times Book Review, September 21, 1924, p. 7.

C62 *Chinese Painting as Reflected in the Thought and Art of Li Lung-Mien: 1070–1106*. by Agnes E. Meyer. New York: Duffield and Co.
New Republic, XL (October 1, 1924), part II, 9–11.

C63 *Latitudes*. by Edwin Muir. New York: B. W. Huebsch.
New Republic, XL (October 29, 1924), 232–33.

C64 *American Social History, as Recorded by British Travellers*. edited by Allan Nevins. New York: Henry Holt & Co.
New Republic, XL (November 12, 1924), 277–78.

C65 *Speculations*. by T. E. Hulme. edited by Herbert Read. New York: Harcourt, Brace and Co.
New Republic, XLI (December 10, 1924), Winter literary section, 11–13.

C66 *The Masters of Modern Art*. by Walter Pach. New York: B. W. Huebsch.
New Republic, XLI (December 17, 1924), 99–100.

C67 *Everyday Architecture: A Sequence of Essays Addressed to the Public.* by Manning Robertson. With an introduction by H. R. Selley. New York: McDevitt-Wilson's.
The Pleasures of Architecture. by C. and A. Williams-Ellis. New York: Houghton Mifflin.
New York Times Book Review, December 21, 1924, p. 15.

1925

C68 *Pipers and a Dancer.* by Stella Benson. New York: Macmillan Co.
Some Do Not. by Ford Maddox Ford. New York: Thomas Seltzer.
New Republic, XLI (January 21, 1925), 241.

C69 *Troubadour.* by Alfred Kreymborg. New York: Boni and Liveright.
New Republic, XLII (April 15, 1925), part II, 11–12.

C70 *The Economic Laws of Art Production.* by Sir Hubert Llewelyn Smith. New York: Oxford University Press.
New York Herald Tribune Books, April 26, 1925, p. 4.

C71 *Art Studies: Medieval, Renaissance and Modern.* by Harvard and Princeton Universities, Departments of Fine Arts. Princeton: Princeton University Press.
An Artist in America. by Maxwell Armfield. London: Methuen and Co.
Gaston Lachaise. by A. E. Gallatin. New York: E. P. Dutton & Co.
The Nature, Practice, and History of Art. by H. Van Buren Magonigle. New York: Charles Scribner's Sons.
One Hundred Drawings. by Abraham Walkowitz. New York: B. W. Huebsch.
New Republic, XLIII (June 17, 1925), 107.

Art Studies: Medieval, Renaissance and Modern was an annual publication. See Book Reviews for 1926 for Mumford's review of the annual of that year.

C72 *He Was a Man.* by Rose Wilder Lane. New York: Harper & Bros.
Love. by "Elizabeth." New York: Doubleday, Page and Co.
The Mulberry Bush. by Sylvia Lynd. New York: Minton, Balch.
Young Mrs. Cruse. by Viola Meynell. New York: Harcourt, Brace and Co.
New Republic, XLIII (June 24, 1925), 132–33.

C73 *The History of American Idealism.* by Gustavus Myers. New York: Boni and Liveright.
Saturday Review of Literature, II (August 22, 1925), 58–59.

C74   *The Super City.* by Robert R. Kern. Washington, D.C.: Privately printed.
      New Republic, XLIV (September 2, 1925), 50–51.

C75   *Bertram Grosvenor Goodhue: Architect and Master of Many Arts.* edited by Charles H. Whitaker. New York: Press of the American Institute of Architects.
      New Republic, XLIV (October 28, 1925), 259–60.

C76   *Emotion in Art.* by Claude Phillips. edited by Maurice W. Brockwell. New York: Houghton Mifflin.
      New York Herald Tribune Books, November 8, 1925, p. 4.

C77   *The Conduct of Life.* by Benedetto Croce. Translated by Arthur Livingston. New York: Harcourt, Brace and Co.
      New Republic, XLV (December 2, 1925), 58–59.

C78   *The Touchstone of Architecture.* by Sir Reginald Blomfield. New York: Oxford University Press.
      New Republic, XLV (December 9, 1925), 92.

1926

C79   *Letters from England.* by Karel Capek. New York: Doubleday, Page and Co.
      New Republic, XLV (January 6, 1926), 196.

C80   *The Pluralist Philosophies of England and America.* by Jean Wahl. London: Open Court Publishing Co.
      New Republic, XLV (January 13, 1926), 225.

C81   *Isabella Stewart Gardner and Fenway Court.* by Morris Carter. New York: Houghton Mifflin.
      New York Herald Tribune Books, January 17, 1926, p. 15.

C82   *Mr. Tasker's Gods.* by T. F. Powys. New York: Alfred A. Knopf. *Mockery Gap.* by T. F. Powys. New York: Alfred A. Knopf.
      New Republic, XLVI (February 24, 1926), 25.

C83   *The Decline of the West.* Vol. I: *Form and Actuality.* by Oswald Spengler. Authorized translation by Charles F. Atkinson. New York: Alfred A. Knopf.
      New Republic, XLVI (May 12, 1926), 367–69.

      Vol. II reviewed in 1929.

C84   *The Dance over Fire and Water.* by Elie Faure. Authorized translation by John Gould Fletcher. New York: Harper & Bros.
      New Republic, XLVII (June 9, 1926), 95.

C85   *Art through the Ages; An Introduction to Its History and Significance.* by Helen Gardner. New York: Harcourt, Brace and Co.
Art Studies: Medieval, Renaissance and Modern. by Harvard and Princeton Universities, Departments of Fine Arts. Cambridge, Mass.: Harvard University Press.
New Republic, XLVII (July 14, 1926), 235–36.

Art Studies: Medieval, Renaissance and Modern was an annual publication. See Book Reviews for 1925 for Mumford's review of the annual of that year.

C86   *The Magnificent Idler.* by Cameron Rogers. New York: Doubleday, Page and Co.
Two Prefaces. by Walt Whitman. New York: Doubleday, Page and Co.
Walt Whitman. by John Bailey. New York: Macmillan Co.
New Republic, XLVII (July 28, 1926), 287–88.

C87   *Dostoevsky.* by André Gide. New York: Alfred A. Knopf.
Dostoevsky Portrayed by His Wife: The Diary and Reminiscences of Mme. Dostoevsky. by A. G. Dostoevsky. Translated and edited by S. S. Koteliansky. New York: E. P. Dutton & Co.
New Republic, XLVII (August 11, 1926), 340–41.

C88   *The American Spirit in Architecture.* by Talbot F. Hamlin. Vol. 13, *The Pageant of America.* New Haven: Yale University Press.
American Institute of Architects. Journal, XIV (September 1926), 410–11.

C89   *Van Gogh.* by Paul Colin. New York: Dodd, Mead and Co.
Corot. by Marc Lafargue. New York: Dodd, Mead and Co.
New Republic, XLVIII (September 8, 1926), 77.

C90   *Herman Melville.* by John Freeman. New York: Macmillan Co.
Swinburne. by Harold Nicolson. New York: Macmillan Co.
New Republic, XLVIII (September 29, 1926), 166–67.

C91   *A Bucolic Attitude.* by Walter P. Eaton. New York: Duffield and Co.
The Freedom of the City. by Charles D. Lay. New York: Duffield and Co.
New Republic, XLVIII (October 27, 1926), 280.

C92   *Whitman: An Interpretation in Narrative.* by Emory Holloway. New York: Alfred A. Knopf.
New York Herald Tribune Books, November 7, 1926, p. 5.

C93 *The Children's Own Book of Letters and Stories.* by Maude B. Harding. Boston: Marshall, Jones Co.
Creative Youth: How a School Environment Set Free the Creative Spirit. by Hughes Mearns. New York: Doubleday, Page and Co.
David Goes to Greenland. by David B. Putnam. New York: G. P. Putnam's Sons.
Deric in Mesa Verde. by Deric Nusbaum. New York: G. P. Putnam's Sons.
New Republic, XLVIII (November 10, 1926), 351–52.

C94 *Time Exposures: Being Portraits of Twenty-One Men and Women Famous in Our Day, Together with Caricatures of the Same by Divers Artists, etc.* by Search-light. New York: Boni and Liveright.
New York Herald Tribune Books, November 21, 1926, p. 7.

C95 *Evolution in Modern Art.* by Frank Rutter. New York: Dial Press.
Primitive Negro Sculpture. by Paul Guillaume and Thomas Munro. New York: Harcourt, Brace and Co.
New Republic, XLIX (December 1, 1926), 49.

1927

C96 *The Book of Marriage: A New Interpretation by Twenty-Four Leaders of Contemporary Thought.* edited by Herman Keyserling. New York: Harcourt, Brace and Co.
New Republic, XLIX (February 9, 1927), 334–35.

C97 *Crashing Thunder: The Autobiography of an American Indian.* edited by Paul Radin. New York: D. Appleton and Co.
New Republic, XLIX (February 16, 1927), 363–64.

C98 *William Blake.* by Osbert Burdett. New York: Macmillan Co.
New Republic, L (May 4, 1927), 306–07.

C99 *A Nation Plan.* by Cyrus Kehr. New York: Oxford University Press.
Saturday Review of Literature, III (May 7, 1927), 800.

C100 *The Rise of American Civilization.* 2 vols. by Charles A. and Mary R. Beard. New York: Macmillan Co.
New Republic, L (May 11, 1927), 338–39.

C101 *Manhattan: The Magical Island: One Hundred and Eight Pictures of Manhattan.* Prelude and descriptive notes by Ben Judah Lubschez. New York: Press of the American Institute of Architects.
New Republic, LI (July 20, 1927), 234–35.

C102 *The Octagon Library of Early American Architecture.* Vol. I: *Charleston, South Carolina.* edited by Albert Simons and Samuel Lapham, Jr. New York: Press of the American Institute of Architects.
New Republic, LI (August 3, 1927), 288–89.

C103 *The Heart of Thoreau's Journals.* edited by Odell Shepard. New York: Houghton Mifflin.
Henry Thoreau: The Cosmic Yankee. by J. Brooks Atkinson. New York: Alfred A. Knopf.
Walden, or Life in the Woods. by Henry David Thoreau. With sixteen woodcuts by Eric Fitch Daglish. New York: Houghton Mifflin.
Robert Frost: A Study in Sensibility and Good Sense. by Gordon H. Munson. New York: George H. Doran Co.
New York Herald Tribune Books, November 6, 1927, p. 1+.

C104 *The Letters of Vincent van Gogh to His Brother: 1872–1886.* With a memoir by his sister-in-law, J. van Gogh-Bonger. Boston: Houghton Mifflin.
New York Herald Tribune Books, November 13, 1927, p. 1+.

C105 *The Children's Book of American Landmarks.* by Lorinda M. Bryant. New York: Century Co.
Wonder Tales of Architecture. by L. Lamprey. New York: F. A. Stokes.
New Republic, LII (November 16, 1927), 361.

C106 *Lazarus Laughed: A Play for an Imaginative Theater.* by Eugene O'Neill. New York: Boni and Liveright.
New York Herald Tribune Books, November 20, 1927, p. 1+.

C107 *Democratic Distinction in America.* by W. C. Brownell. New York: Charles Scribner's Sons.
Prejudices: Sixth Series. by H. L. Mencken. New York: Alfred A. Knopf.
New York Herald Tribune Books, November 27, 1927, p. 1+.

1928

C108 *Charles Darwin.* by Leonard Huxley. New York: Greenberg.
Charles Darwin: The Man and His Warfare. by Henshaw Ward. Indianapolis, Ind.: Bobbs, Merrill Co.
Darwin. by Gamaliel Bradford. Boston: Houghton Mifflin.

The Evolution of Charles Darwin. by George A. Dorsey. New York: Doubleday, Page and Co.
New Republic, LIII (February 1, 1928), 301–02.

C109 *Time and Western Man.* by Wyndham Lewis. New York: Harcourt, Brace and Co.
New Republic, LIV (March 7, 1928), 102–03.

C110 *George Meredith.* by J. B. Priestley. New York: Macmillan Co.
Thomas Love Peacock. by J. B. Priestley. New York: Macmillan Co.
New Republic, LIV (March 28, 1928), 199–200.

C111 *Life and the Student.* by Charles Horton Cooley. New York: Alfred A. Knopf.
New Republic, LIV (April 4, 1928), 226–27.

C112 *The Mind and Face of Bolshevism: An Examination of Cultural Life in Soviet Russia.* by René Fülöp-Miller. Translated from the German by S. Flint and D. F. Tait. New York: Alfred A. Knopf.
New Republic, LIV (April 11, 1928), 250–51.

C113 *Cézanne.* by Roger Fry. New York: Macmillan Co.
Cézanne. by Julius Meier-Graefe. Translated by J. Holroyd-Reece. New York: Charles Scribner's Sons.
New Republic, LIV (May 2, 1928), 331.

C114 *The Intelligent Woman's Guide to Socialism and Capitalism.* by Bernard Shaw. New York: Brentano's.
New Republic, LV (July 4, 1928), 177–78.

C115 *American Criticism: A Study in Literary Theory from Poe to the Present.* by Norman Foerster. Boston: Houghton Mifflin.
New Republic, LVI (August 29, 1928), 50–51.

C116 *Spokesmen: Modern Writers and American Life.* by T. K. Whipple. New York: D. Appleton and Co.
New Republic, LVI (September 5, 1928), 77–78.

C117 *Life of Charles Dickens.* by John Forster. New York: Doubleday, Doran and Co.
Charles Dickens: A Biography from New Sources. by Ralph Straus. New York: Cosmopolitan Book Corp.
Zola and His Time. by Matthew Josephson. New York: Macauley Co.

Elizabeth and Essex. by Lytton Strachey. New York: Harcourt, Brace and Co.

Pieter Stuyvesant and His Times. by Hendrik Willem Van Loon. New York: Henry Holt and Co.

Bonnet and Shawl: An Album. by Philip Guedella. New York: G. P. Putnam's Sons.

The Early Life of Thomas Hardy. by Florence E. Hardy. New York: Macmillan Co.

William Dean Howells: Life in Letters. edited by Mildred Howells. New York: Doubleday, Doran and Co.

    Atlantic Monthly, CXLII (December 1928), 20+.

1929

C118 *Further Poems of Emily Dickinson.* edited by her niece, Martha Dickinson Bianchi and Alfred Leete Hampson. Boston: Little, Brown and Co.

    New York Herald Tribune Books, March 17, 1929, p. 1+.

C119 *The Decline of the West.* Vol. II: *Perspectives of World History.* by Oswald Spengler. Authorized translation by Charles F. Atkinson. New York: Alfred A. Knopf.

    New Republic, LVIII (March 20, 1929), 140–41.

    Vol. I reviewed in 1926.

C120 *Bitter Bierce. A Mystery of American Letters.* by C. Hartley Grattan. Garden City, N.Y.: Doubleday, Doran and Co.

Portrait of Ambrose Bierce. by Adolphe de Castro. New York: Century Co.

    New York Herald Tribune Books, March 24, 1929, p. 1+.

C121 *The Re-Discovery of America: An Introduction to a Philosophy of American Life.* by Waldo Frank. New York: Charles Scribner's Sons.

    New York Herald Tribune Books, March 31, 1929, p. 1+.

C122 *Frank Lloyd Wright.* by Henry-Russell Hitchcock. Paris: Editions "Cahiers d'Art."

    Architectural Record, LXV (April 1929), 414–16.

C123 *Medieval Culture. An Introduction to Dante and His Times.* 2 vols. by Karl Vossler. Translated by William Cranston Lawton. New York: Harcourt, Brace and Co.

    New York Herald Tribune Books, April 7, 1929, p. 1+.

C124 *Roundup. The Stories of Ring W. Lardner.* by Ring W. Lardner. New York: Charles Scribner's Sons.
New York Herald Tribune Books, April 14, 1929, p. 5.

C125 *The Modern Temper; A Study and Confession.* by Joseph Wood Krutch. New York: Harcourt, Brace and Co.
New Republic, LIX (May 22, 1929), 36–38.

C126 *The Life of George Meredith.* by Robert Esmonde Sencourt. New York: Charles Scribner's Sons.
New Republic, LX (November 13, 1929), 355–56.

C127 *Mrs Eddy: The Biography of a Virginal Mind.* by Edwin Franden Dakin. New York: Charles Scribner's Sons.
New Republic, LXI (November 27, 1929), 21–22.

C128 *The Gothick North: A Study of Medieval Life, Art, and Thought.* by Sacheverell Sitwell. Boston: Houghton Mifflin.
Saturday Review of Literature, VI (November 30, 1929), 475.

C129 *Essays in Philosophy.* edited by Thomas Vernor Smith and William Kelley Wright. Chicago: Open Court Publishing Co.
The Philosophic Way of Life. by Thomas Vernor Smith. Chicago: University of Chicago Press.
Process and Reality: An Essay in Cosmology. by Alfred North Whitehead. New York: Macmillan Co.
New Republic, LXI (December 18, 1929), 117–18.

1930

C130 *The City of Tomorrow and Its Planning.* by Le Corbusier. Translated by Frederic Etchells. New York: Payson and Clarke.
The Metropolis of Tomorrow. by Hugh Ferris. New York: Ives Washburn.
Our Cities Today and Tomorrow; A Survey of Planning and Zoning Progress in the United States. by Theodore Kimball Hubbard and Henry Vincent. Cambridge: Harvard University Press.
New Republic, LXI (February 12, 1930), 332–33.

For Mumford's reply to criticism of the review of Ferris's book, see *New Republic,* LXII (April 23, 1930), 275.

C131 *Art in America.* by Suzanne La Follette. New York: Harper & Bros.
New Republic, LXII (March 5, 1930), 77.

86   C. BOOK REVIEWS

C132 *Modern Architecture; Romanticism and Reintegration.* by Henry-Russell Hitchcock. New York: Payson and Clarke.
   New Republic, LXII (March 19, 1930), 131–32.

C133 *Humanism and America; Essays on the Outlook of Modern Civilization.* edited by Norman Foerster. New York: Farrar and Rinehart.
   New Republic, LXII (March 26, 1930), 162.

C134 *The Function of Reason.* Louis Clark Vanuxem Foundation Lectures. by Alfred North Whitehead. Princeton: Princeton University Press.
   The Sciences and Philosophy. Gifford Lectures, University of Glasgow, 1927–28. by J. S. Haldane. New York: Doubleday, Doran and Co.
   New Republic, LXII (May 7, 1930), 331–32.

C135 *Toward Civilization.* edited by Charles A. Beard. New York: Longmans, Green and Co.
   New Republic, LXIII (May 28, 1930), 49–50.

C136 *A History of Modern Culture.* Vol. I: *The Great Renewal, 1543–1687.* by Preserved Smith. New York: Henry Holt & Co.
   New Republic, LXIII (July 9, 1930), 210–11.

   Vol. II reviewed in 1934.

C137 *Science and the New Civilization.* by Robert A. Millikan. New York: Charles Scribner's Sons.
   New Republic, LXIII (August 6, 1930), 348–49.

C138 *R. v. R., the Life and Times of Rembrandt van Rijn.* by Hendrik W. Van Loon. New York: Horace Liveright.
   New Freeman, II (December 17, 1930), 331.

   1931

C139 *American Critical Essays.* edited by Norman Foerster. New York: Oxford University Press.
   Towards Standards. by Norman Foerster. New York: Farrar and Rinehart.
   New Republic, LXV (January 14, 1931), 249–50.

C140 *Folk-Say; A Regional Miscellany.* edited by B. A. Botkin. Norman, Okla.: University of Oklahoma Press.
   New Republic, LXVI (March 25, 1931), 157–58.

C141 *Men of Art.* by Thomas Craven. New York: Simon and Schuster.
  New York Herald Tribune Books, March 29, 1931, p. 1+.

C142 *The Genteel Tradition at Bay.* by George Santayana. New York: Charles Scribner's Sons.
  New Republic, LXVI (April 8, 1931), 214.

C143 *Looking Backward, 2000–1887.* by Edward Bellamy. Boston: Houghton Mifflin.
  New Republic, LXVIII (August 26, 1931), 51–52.

C144 *Life; Outlines of General Biology.* 2 vols. by Patrick Geddes and J. Arthur Thomson. New York: Harper & Bros.
  New Republic, LXVIII (September 16, 1931), 130–31.

C145 *The Scientific Outlook.* by Bertrand Russell. New York: W. W. Norton and Co.
  New Republic, LXVIII (October 28, 1931), 303–04.

1932

C146 *The Literary Mind; Its Place in an Age of Science.* by Max Eastman. New York: Charles Scribner's Sons.
  New Republic, LXIX (February 3, 1932), 329.

C147 *Man and Technics; A Contribution to a Philosophy of Life.* by Oswald Spengler. Translated by Charles Francis Atkinson. New York: Alfred A. Knopf.
  New Republic, LXX (March 9, 1932), 104.

1933

C148 *A Cultural History of the Modern Age.* Vol. III: *The Crisis of the European Soul from the Black Death to the World War.* by Egon Friedell. Translated from the German by Charles Francis Atkinson. New York: Alfred A. Knopf.
  New Republic, LXXIII (January 11, 1933), 248–49.

C149 *Town and Countryside; Some Aspects of Urban and Rural Development.* by Thomas Sharp. New York: Oxford University Press.
  New Republic, LXXIV (May 3, 1933), 343–44.

C150 *The Ordeal of Mark Twain.* Revised edition. by Van Wyck Brooks. New York: E. P. Dutton & Co.
  Saturday Review of Literature, IX (May 6, 1933), 573–75.

C151 *A Century of Progress.* edited by Charles A. Beard. New York: Harper & Bros.
New Republic, LXXVI (September 6, 1933), 106–07.

C152 *The Evolving House; A History of the Home.* by Albert F. Bemis and John Burchard, 2d. Cambridge, Mass.: The Technology Press.
New Republic, LXXVI (September 20, 1933), 164–65.

Mumford replies to criticism of this review in *New Republic,* LXXVI (October 18, 1933), 283.

C153 John Day Pamphlets:
The Promise of Power. by Stuart Chase.
A Call to the Teachers of the Nation. by Committee on Social and Economic Problems of the Progressive Education Association.
The Farmer Is Doomed. by Louis M. Hacker.
Instead of Dictatorship. by Henry Hazlitt.
Nazi Culture. by Matthew Josephson.
A New Social Order. by Walter Lippmann.
Work Camps for America. by Osgood Nichols and Comstock Glaser.
New York: John Day Company.
New Republic, LXXVI (October 11, 1933), 249.

C154 *The Power Age; Its Quest and Challenge.* by Walter N. Polakov. New York: Covici-Friede.
New Republic, LXXVII (December 6, 1933), 107.

1934

C155 *The Hour of Decision.* Part I: *Germany and World-Historical Evolution.* by Oswald Spengler. New York: Alfred A. Knopf.
New Republic, LXXVIII (February 21, 1934), 51–52.

C156 *A History of Modern Culture.* Vol. II: *The Enlightenment, 1687–1776.* by Preserved Smith. New York: Henry Holt & Co.
New Republic, LXXX (September 19, 1934), 167.

Vol. I reviewed in 1930.

C157 *A Free Society.* by Horace M. Kallen. New York: Robert O. Ballou.
New Republic, LXXX (October 3, 1934), 222–23.

Mumford replies to criticism of this review in *New Republic,* LXXXI (December 5, 1934), 105.

C158 *Freedom and Organization, 1814–1914.* by Bertrand Russell. New York: W. W. Norton and Co.
New Republic, LXXX (October 17, 1934), 277–78.

1935

C159 *Thorstein Veblen and His America.* by Joseph Dorfman. New York: Viking Press.
Saturday Review of Literature, XI (January 12, 1935), 417+.

C160 *Social Judgment.* by Graham Wallas. New York: Harcourt, Brace and Co.
New Republic, LXXXII (April 17, 1935), 293.

C161 *Capitalism and Its Culture.* by Jerome Davis. New York: Farrar and Rinehart.
New Republic, LXXXIII (July 10, 1935), 258.

C162 *Quack, Quack!* by Leonard Woolf. New York: Harcourt, Brace and Co.
New Republic, LXXXIV (October 23, 1935), 308.

C163 *The Sociology of Invention.* by S. C. Gilfillan. Chicago: Follett Publishing Co.
New Republic, LXXXV (November 13, 1935), 25.

C164 *Poor John Fitch: Inventor of the Steamboat.* by Thomas Boyd. New York: G. P. Putnam's Sons.
New Republic, LXXXV (November 27, 1935), 82.

C165 *A Study of History.* Vols. I–III. by Arnold Toynbee. New York: Oxford University Press.
New Republic, LXXXV (November 27, 1935), 63–66.

Vols. IV–VI reviewed in 1940, Vols. VII–X reviewed in 1954.

1936

C166 *The Architecture of H. H. Richardson and His Times, 1838–1886.* by Henry-Russell Hitchcock. New York: Museum of Modern Art. *Louis Sullivan: Prophet of Modern Architecture.* by Hugh Morrison. New York: W. W. Norton and Co.
New Republic, LXXXVI (February 26, 1936), 87–88.

C167 *Studies in the Psychology of Sex.* 4 vols. by Havelock Ellis. New York: Random House.
New Republic, LXXXVI (April 15, 1936), 281–82.

C168 *Men of Science.* by J. G. Crowther. New York: W. W. Norton and Co.
   New Republic, LXXXVII (June 3, 1936), 108.

C169 *In the Shadow of Tomorrow.* by Jan Huizinga. New York: W. W. Norton and Co.
   New Republic, LXXXVIII (September 30, 1936), 230–31.

1937

C170 *Anarchy and Hierarchy.* by Salvador de Madariaga. New York: Macmillan Co.
   New Republic, XCI (June 9, 1937), 135–36.

C171 *Social and Cultural Dynamics.* 3 vols. by Pitrim A. Sorokin. New York: American Book Co.
   New Republic, XCI (July 14, 1937), 283–84.

C172 *An Inquiry into the Principles of the Great Society.* by Walter Lippmann. Boston: Little, Brown and Co.
   New Republic, XCII (September 29, 1937), 219–20.

C173 Federal Writers' Project Guides:
   Massachusetts: A Guide to Its Places and People.
   Vermont: A Guide to the Green Mountain State.
   Dutchess County.
   Intercoastal Waterway, Norfolk to Key West.
   Cape Cod Pilot.
   New Republic, XCII (October 20, 1937), 306–07.

1938

C174 *American Stuff: An Anthology of Prose and Verse.* by members of the Federal Writers' Project. New York: Viking Press.
   New Republic, XCIII (January 12, 1938), 289.

C175 *Walt Whitman's Pose.* by Esther Shephard. New York: Harcourt, Brace and Co.
   New Republic, XCV (May 11, 1938), 23–24.

C176 *The Conquest of Culture.* by M. D. C. Crawford. New York: Greenberg.
   New Republic, XCVI (August 31, 1938), 110–11.

1939

C177 *The New Western Front.* by Stuart Chase. New York: Harcourt, Brace and Co.
   New York Post, April 17, 1939, p. 8.

C178 *My Life: Autobiography of Havelock Ellis.* Boston: Houghton Mifflin.
  New Republic, CI (December 20, 1939), 265–66.

1940

C179 *A Study of History.* Vols. IV–VI. by Arnold Toynbee. New York: Oxford University Press.
  New Republic, CII (April 1, 1940), 445–46.

  Vols. I–III reviewed in 1935, Vols. VII–X reviewed in 1954.

C180 *The Museum in America: A Critical Study.* 3 vols. by Lawrence V. Coleman. Washington: American Association of Museums.
  City College Alumnus (N.Y.), XXXVI (October 1940), 92.

1941

C181 *Architecture through the Ages.* by Talbot F. Hamlin. New York: G. P. Putnam's Sons.
  Art Bulletin: A Quarterly Published by the College Art Association of America, XXIII (March 1941), 86–87.

1942

C182 *Defense Will Not Win the War.* by W. F. Kernan. Boston: Little, Brown and Co.
  New Republic, CVI (March 16, 1942), 373.

C183 *The Roots of American Culture.* by Constance Rourke. edited with a preface by Van Wyck Brooks. New York: Harcourt, Brace and Co.
  Saturday Review of Literature, XXV (August 15, 1942), 3–4.

C184 *A Time for Greatness.* by Herbert Agar. Boston: Little, Brown and Co.
  Atlantic Monthly, CLXX (November 1942), 134.

1943

C185 *Can Our Cities Survive? An ABC of Urban Problems, Their Analysis, Their Solutions.* by José Luis Sert. Cambridge, Mass.: Harvard University Press.
  New Republic, CVIII (February 8, 1943), 186–87.

C186 *South American Journey.* by Waldo Frank. New York: Duell, Sloan and Pearce.
  New York Times Book Review, May 23, 1943, p. 5.

Additional discussion of this book in Mumford's later essay "Lewis Mumford Pays Tribute to Waldo Frank," in *New York Times Book Review*, September 5, 1943, p. 4+.

1944

C187 *Greek Revival Architecture in America.* by Talbot Hamlin. London: Oxford University Press.
  William and Mary Quarterly, third series, I (October 1944), 413–17.

1945

C188 *Herman Melville; The Tragedy of Mind.* by William E. Sedgewick. Cambridge, Mass.: Harvard University Press.
  New York Times Book Review, January 21, 1945, p. 3.

C189 *Beyond All Fronts.* by Max Jordan. Milwaukee, Wisc.: Bruce Publishing Co.
  Civil Life in Wartime Germany. by Max Seydewitz. New York: Viking Press.
  The German Record. by William Ebenstein. New York: Farrar and Rinehart.
  Germany, A Short History. by George N. Shuster and Arnold Bergstraesser. New York: W. W. Norton and Co.
  Germany after Hitler. by Paul Hagen. New York: Farrar and Rinehart.
  Germany: To Be or Not To Be? by Gerhart H. Seger and Siegfried K. Marck. New York: Rand School Press.
  Prelude to Silence. by Arnold Brecht. New York: Oxford University Press.
  Re-Educating Germany. by Werner Richter. Translated by Paul Lehmann. Chicago: University of Chicago Press.
  The Tyrants' War and the Peoples' Peace. by Ferdinand A. Hermens. Chicago: University of Chicago Press.
  Saturday Review of Literature, XXVIII (August 11, 1945), 5–6+.

Mumford replies to criticism of these reviews in the same volume, issue of October 6, 1945, pages 17–18.

C190 *The German Talks Back.* by Heinrich Hauser. New York: Henry Holt & Co.
  Saturday Review of Literature, XXVIII (September 22, 1945), 9–10.

C191 *One Destiny.* by Sholem Asch. New York: G. P. Putnam's Sons.
Saturday Review of Literature, XXVIII (September 29, 1945),
12.

1946

C192 *The Case against the Nazi War Criminals.* Opening statement for
the United States of America by Robert H. Jackson and other documents. New York: Alfred A. Knopf.
Saturday Review of Literature, XXIX (March 16, 1946), 13–14.

1947

C193 *The Future of Housing.* by Charles Abrams. New York: Harper
& Bros.
Survey Graphic, XXXVI (February 1947), 166–67.

C194 *Call Me Ishmael.* by Charles Olson. New York: Reynal and Hitchcock.
New York Times Book Review, April 6, 1947, p. 4.

C195 *When the Cathedrals Were White.* by Le Corbusier. New York:
Reynal and Hitchcock.
Communitas; Ways of Livelihood and Ways of Life. by Paul and
Percival Goodman. Chicago: University of Chicago Press.
Virginia Quarterly Review, XXIII (Summer 1947), 439–43.

C196 *The Times of Melville and Whitman.* by Van Wyck Brooks. New
York: E. P. Dutton and Co.
Saturday Review of Literature, XXX (November 8, 1947), 11–
13.

1948

C197 *City, Region and Regionalism: A Geographical Contribution to
Human Ecology.* by Robert E. Dickinson. London: Kegan Paul,
Trench, Trubner and Co.
Architectural Review, CIII (January 1948), 31.

C198 *The Next Development in Man.* by Lancelot Law Whyte. New
York: Henry Holt and Co.
Saturday Review of Literature, XXXI (April 24, 1948), 22–24.

C199 *Mechanization Takes Command: A Contribution to Anonymous
History.* by Sigfried Giedion. New York: Oxford University Press.
Progressive Architecture, XXIX (July 1948), 48+.

1949

C200 *The Reconstruction of Humanity.* by Pitrim A. Sorokin. Boston: Beacon Press.
  Journal of Religion, XXIX (October 1949), 301–02.

1950

C201 *Backwoods Utopia: The Sectarian and Owenite Phases of Communitarian Socialism in America, 1663–1829.* by Arthur E. Bestor, Jr. Philadelphia: University of Pennsylvania Press.
  William and Mary Quarterly, 3d series, VII (October 1950), 620–22.

C202 *A Plan for Peace.* by Grenville Clark. New York: Harper & Bros.
  Saturday Review of Literature, XXXIII (November 25, 1950), 13–14.

1954

C203 *A Study of History.* Vols. VII–X. by Arnold Toynbee. New York: Oxford University Press.
  New Republic, CXXXI (November 8, 1954), 15–18.

  Vols. I–III reviewed in 1935, Vols. IV–VI reviewed in 1940.

1955

C204 *The American City Novel.* by Blanche Gelfant. Norman: University of Oklahoma Press.
  American Quarterly, VII (Spring 1955), 76+.

1956

C205 *A History of Technology.* Vol. I: *From Early Times to the Fall of the Ancient Empires.* edited by Charles J. Singer, et al. New York: Oxford University Press.
  New Yorker, XXXI (January 14, 1956), 100–02+.

  Vol. II reviewed in 1958, Vols. III–V reviewed in 1960.

C206 *American Skyline.* by Christopher Tunnard and Henry H. Reed. Boston: Houghton Mifflin.
  Cities in Revolt. by Carl Bridenbaugh. New York: Alfred A. Knopf.
  Great Cities of the World, Their Government, Politics, and Planning. edited by William A. Robson. New York: Macmillan Co.
  New Yorker, XXXII (March 3, 1956), 114+.

1957

C207 *Sydney's Great Experiment: The Progress of the Cumberland County Plan.* by Dennis Winston. Sydney, Australia: Angus and Robertson.
 Progressive Architecture, XXXVIII (November 1957), 284+.

1958

C208 *A History of Technology.* Vol. II: *The Mediterranean Civilizations and the Middle Ages.* edited by Charles J. Singer, et al. New York: Oxford University Press.
 New Yorker, XXXIV (September 27, 1958), 165–70+.

Vol. I reviewed in 1956, Vols. III–V reviewed in 1960.

This review and the one that appeared in 1956 were republished in *Technology and Culture,* I (Fall 1960), 320–34.

1959

C209 *George Perkins Marsh: Versatile Vermonter.* by David Lowenthal. New York: Columbia University Press.
 Living Wilderness, Winter 1959–60, pp. 11–13.

1960

C210 *Can Man Plan? and Other Verses.* by Frederic J. Osborn. London: G. G. Harrap.
 Town and Country Planning, XXVIII (March 1960), 115.

C211 *A History of Technology.* Vol. III: *From the Renaissance to the Industrial Revolution.* Vol. IV: *The Industrial Revolution, c. 1750 to c. 1850.* Vol. V: *The Late Nineteenth Century, c. 1850 to c. 1900.* edited by Charles J. Singer, et al. New York: Oxford University Press.
 New Yorker, XXXVI (October 8, 1960), 180+.

Vol. I reviewed in 1956, Vol. II reviewed in 1958.

1961

C212 *The Preindustrial City; Past and Present.* by Gideon Sjoberg. Glencoe, Ill.: Free Press.
 American Sociological Review, XXVI (August 1961), 656–57.

1963

C213 *Courses toward Urban Life.* by Robert J. Braidwood and Gordon R. Willey. Chicago: Aldine Publishing Co.
 Landscape, XII (Spring 1963), 14–16.

1964

C214 *The Time of "The Dial."* by William Wasserstrom. Syracuse: Syracuse University Press.
A "Dial" Miscellany. edited by William Wasserstrom. Syracuse: Syracuse University Press.
New York Review of Books, II (February 20, 1964), 3–5.

C215 *Memories, Dreams, Reflections.* by Carl G. Jung. New York: Pantheon Books.
New Yorker, XL (May 23, 1964), 155–56+.

1965

C216 *The Eternal Present, A Contribution on Constancy and Change.* Vol. I: *Beginnings of Art.* Vol. II: *Beginnings of Architecture.* by Sigfried Giedion. New York: Pantheon Books.
New Yorker, XLI (March 6, 1965), 158+.

C217 *Garden Cities of Tomorrow.* by Ebenezer Howard. edited, with a preface, by F. J. Osborn. With an introductory essay by Lewis Mumford. Cambridge, Mass.: M.I.T. Press.
New York Review of Books, IV (April 8, 1965), 10–12.

C218 *Religions, Values, and Peak-Experiences.* by Abraham Maslow. Columbus, Ohio: Ohio State University Press.
Journal of Humanistic Psychology, V (Fall 1965), 229–32.

1966

C219 *Unsafe at Any Speed.* by Ralph Nader. New York: Grossman.
Safety Last. by Jeffrey O'Connell and Arthur Myers. New York: Random House.
New York Review of Books, VI (April 28, 1966), 3–5.

C220 *The Original Water-color Paintings by John James Audubon for "The Birds of America."* 2 vols. From the New York Historical Society. American Heritage.
John James Audubon: A Biography. by Alexander B. Adams. New York: G. P. Putnam's Sons.
New York Review of Books, VII (December 1, 1966), 16+.

1967

C221 *The Urgent Future; People, Housing, City, Region.* by Albert Mayer. New York: McGraw-Hill Book Co.
Architectural Record, CXLII (December 1967), 131–34.

1968

C222 *The Early Lectures of Ralph Waldo Emerson.* 2 vols. edited by Robert E. Spiller and Stephen E. Whicher. Cambridge, Mass.: Harvard University Press.
The Journals and Miscellaneous Notebooks of Ralph Waldo Emerson. 6 vols. edited by William H. Gilman, et al. Cambridge, Mass.: Belknap Press, Harvard University Press.
New York Review of Books, X (January 18, 1968), 3–5.

For Mumford's replies to reader comment on this review, see *New York Review of Books,* X (March 14, 1968), 36, and (May 23, 1968), 43.

C223 *William Morris as Designer.* by Ray Watkinson. New York: Reinhold Publishing Co.
William Morris: His Life, Work and Friends. by Philip Henderson. New York: McGraw-Hill Book Co.
The Work of William Morris. by Paul Thompson. New York: Viking Press.
New York Review of Books, X (May 23, 1968), 8+.

D. WRITINGS IN CO-OPERATIVE WORKS OR WORKS EDITED BY OTHERS

D1 "The City,"
in *Civilization in the United States; An Inquiry by Thirty Americans*. Edited by Harold S. Stearns. New York: Harcourt, Brace and Co., 1922. pp. 3–20.

Included in the collection of Mumford's essays, *City Development* (1945).

D2 "The Little Testament of Bernard Martin Aet. 30,"
in *The Second American Caravan; A Yearbook of American Literature*. Edited by Alfred Kreymborg, Lewis Mumford, and Paul Rosenfeld. New York: Macaulay Co., 1928. pp. 123–69.

A selection from this short novel is included in the collection of Mumford's essays and other writings, *The Human Prospect* (1955).

D3 "The Arts,"
in *Whither Mankind; A Panorama of Modern Civilization*. Edited by Charles A. Beard. New York: Longmans, Green and Co., 1928. pp. 287–312.

D4 "Architecture: Since the Renaissance,"
in *Encyclopedia of the Social Sciences*. New York: Macmillan Co., 1930. II, 172–75.

D5 "Civic Art,"
in *Encyclopedia of the Social Sciences*. New York: Macmillan Co., 1930. III, 492–94.

D6 "Towards an Organic Humanism,"
in *The Critique of Humanism*. Edited by C. Hartley Grattan. New York: Brewer and Warren, 1930. pp. 337–59.

Appeared originally in somewhat altered form with the title "A Modern Synthesis" in *Saturday Review of Literature*, VI (April 12, 1930), 920–21, and (May 10, 1930), 1028–29.

D7   [Credo,]
in *Living Philosophies.* New York: Simon and Schuster, 1931. pp. 205–19.

Appeared originally in different form in *Forum*, LXXXIV (November 1930), 263–68, with the title "What I Believe."

D8   "Housing,"
in *Modern Architecture.* New York: Museum of Modern Art, 1932. pp. 179–92.

D9   "The Social Imperatives in Housing,"
in *America Can't Have Housing.* Edited by Carol Aronovici. New York: Published for the Committee on the Housing Exhibition by the Museum of Modern Art, 1934. pp. 15–19.

D10   "The Metropolitan Milieu,"
in *America and Alfred Stieglitz; A Collective Portrait.* Edited by Waldo Frank, Lewis Mumford, Dorothy Norman, Paul Rosenfeld and Harold Rugg. Garden City, N.Y.: Doubleday, Doran and Co., 1934. pp. 33–58.

Also published in 1934 as a Literary Guild edition.

Included in two collections of Mumford's essays: *City Development* (1945) and *The Human Prospect* (1955).

D11   [Self Portrait,]
in *Portraits and Self-Portraits.* Collected and illustrated by Georges Schreiber. Boston: Houghton Mifflin Co., 1936. pp. 117–20.

D12   "The Death of the Monument,"
in *Circle; An International Survey of Constructive Art.* Edited by James L. Martin, Ben Nicholson, and N. Gabo. London: Faber and Faber, 1937. pp. 263–70.

From a chapter in Mumford's *The Culture of Cities* (1938).

D13   "Spengler's 'The Decline of the West,' "
in *Books That Changed Our Minds.* Edited by Malcolm Cowley and Bernard Smith. New York: Doubleday, Doran and Co., 1939. pp. 217–35.

Essentially the same essay, somewhat expanded, that appeared in the *New Republic*, XCVII (January 11, 1939), 275–79.

D14   "I Believe,"
in *I Believe; The Personal Philosophies of Certain Eminent Men*

and Women of Our Time. Edited by Clifton Fadiman. New York: Simon and Schuster, 1939. pp. 399–401.

D15 "The Social Responsibilities of Teachers,"
in *Cultural and Social Elements in the Education of Teachers.* Washington: Commission on Teacher Education, American Council on Education; Educational Policies Commission, National Education Association of the United States; American Association of School Administrators, 1940. pp. 21–49.

An address given at the Planning Conference held at Bennington College, August 1939.

Also published with slight changes in *Educational Record,* XX (October 1939), 471–99.

Included in the collection of Mumford's essays, *Values for Survival* (1946).

D16 "The Unified Approach to Knowledge and Life,"
in *University and the Future of America.* Stanford, California: Stanford University Press, 1941. pp. 108–36.

Included in the collection of Mumford's essays, *Values for Survival* (1946).

D17 [Untitled chapter,]
in *Let's Face the Facts.* London: John Lane the Bodley Head, 1941. pp. 171–83.

Originally a speech delivered over the Canadian Broadcasting network, December 1, 1940.

D18 "Looking Forward,"
in *Science and Man.* Edited by Ruth N. Anshen. New York: Harcourt, Brace and Co., 1942. pp. 346–57.

Also published in *This Changing World.* Edited by J. R. M. Brumwell. London: George Routledge & Sons Ltd., 1944.

Not the same essay which appeared with this title in American Philosophical Society. *Proceedings,* LXXXIII (No. 4, 1940), 539–47.

D19 "Address by Lewis Mumford,"
in *World-wide Civil War.* by Herbert Agar, Lewis Mumford, and Frank Kingdon. Report of the Lincoln day meeting. New York: Freedom House, 1942. pp. 10–11.

D20 "The Task of Tomorrow,"
in *New World Theme*. Stanford University, California: J. L. Delkin, 1943. pp. 27–33.

An address given at Stanford University, October 6, 1942.

D21 "The Making of Men,"
in *The Humanities Look Ahead*. Report of the First Annual Conference held by the Stanford School of Humanities. Stanford, California: Stanford University Press, 1943. pp. 131–46.

Included in the collection of Mumford's essays, *Values for Survival* (1946).

D22 "Symposium—'A New Kind of Teacher,'"
in *The Humanities Look Ahead*. Report of the First Annual Conference held by the Stanford School of Humanities. Stanford, California: Stanford University Press, 1943. pp. 127–30.

D23 "Patrick Geddes, Victor Branford, and Applied Sociology in
England: The Urban Survey, Regionalism, and Urban Planning,"
in *An Introduction to the History of Sociology*. Edited by Harry Elmer Barnes. Chicago: University of Chicago Press, 1948. pp. 677–95.

D24 "Lyric Wisdom,"
in *Paul Rosenfeld; Voyager in the Arts*. Edited by Jerome Mellquist and Lucie Wiese. New York: Creative Age Press, 1948. pp. 40–75.

D25 "The Architecture of the Bay Region,"
in *Domestic Architecture of the San Francisco Bay Region*. San Francisco Museum of Art. San Francisco: San Francisco Museum of Art, 1949. 2 pages (unnumbered).

D26 "Ideals for a New Age,"
in *Centennial Addresses; The City College of New York*. New York: The City College Press, 1950. pp. 51–62.

This address delivered April 14, 1947.

D27 "Summary and Synthesis,"
in *The Nature of Man; His World, His Spiritual Resources, His Destiny*. Edited by A. William Loos. New York: The Church Union and the World Alliance for International Friendship through Religion, 1950. pp. 81–87.

D28 "From Revolt to Renewal,"
in *The Arts in Renewal*. by Lewis Mumford and others. Introduc-

tion by Sculley Bradley. Benjamin Franklin Lectures of the University of Pennsylvania, 3d Series, 1950. Philadelphia: University of Pennsylvania Press, 1951. pp. 1–31.

D29 "The Modern City,"
in *Forms and Functions of Twentieth Century Architecture.* Vol. IV: *Building Types.* Edited by Talbot Hamlin. New York: Columbia University Press, 1952. pp. 775–819.

D30 "How Art Education Strengthens Democracy,"
in *This Is Art Education 1952.* 1952 Yearbook of the National Art Education Association. Edited by I. L. de Francesco. pp. 35–48.

D31 "The Conversation in New York,"
in *The Architect at Mid-Century.* Vol. II: *Conversations across the Nation.* Edited by Francis R. Bellamy. New York: Reinhold Publishing Co., 1954. pp. 5–30.

A transcript of a conversation among a group of twelve persons, representing such professions as architecture, teaching, law, and the arts, dealing with the future of America and the kind of professional education our educators must provide young men and women.

D32 "The Art of the 'Impossible,' "
in *Alternatives to the H-Bomb.* by Lewis Mumford and others. A symposium organized by the *New Leader* magazine and edited by Anatole Shub. Boston: Beacon Press, 1955. pp. 12–29.

This essay appeared originally with the title "Alternatives to the H-Bomb" in *New Leader,* XXXVII (June 28, 1954), 4–9.

D33 "The Natural History of Urbanization,"
in *Man's Role in Changing the Face of the Earth.* Edited by William L. Thomas; Symposium under the chairmanship of Carl Sauer, Marston Bates, and Lewis Mumford. Chicago: University of Chicago Press, 1956. pp. 382–98.

D34 "Summary Remarks: Prospect,"
in *Man's Role in Changing the Face of the Earth.* Cited above, pp. 1142–52.

Both of the above were addresses delivered at the International Symposium on "Man's Role in Changing the Face of the Earth," sponsored by the Wenner-Gren Foundation for Anthropological Research, held at Princeton, New Jersey, June 16–21, 1955.

D35 "The Transformations of Man,"
in *Brainpower Quest; A Report on a Convocation Called by the*

Cooper Union for the Advancement of Science and Art to Find New Sources from Which to Draw Tomorrow's Leaders in Science and Engineering. Edited by Andrew A. Freeman. New York: Macmillan Co., 1957. pp. 75–88.

D36 "The Fulfillment of Man,"
in *This Is My Philosophy*. Edited by Whit Burnett. New York: Harper & Bros., 1957. pp. 7–33.

Selections from Mumford's *The Condition of Man* (1944) and *The Conduct of Life* (1951).

D37 "Henry Wright,"
in *Dictionary of American Biography*. New York: Charles Scribner's Sons, 1958. XXII, Supplement Two, 737–39.

D38 "How War Began,"
in *Adventures of the Mind*. Edited by Richard Truelson and John Kobler. Introduction by Mark Van Doren. New York: Alfred Knopf, 1959. pp. 175–89.

Originally published in *Saturday Evening Post*, CCXXXI (April 18, 1959), 24–25+.

D39 "University City,"
in *City Invincible; A Symposium on Urbanization and Cultural Development in the Ancient Near East*. Held at the Oriental Institute of the University of Chicago, December 4–7, 1958. Edited by Carl H. Kraeling and Robert M. Adams. Chicago: University of Chicago Press, 1960. pp. 5–19.

D40 "Concluding Address,"
in *City Invincible*. . . . Cited above, pp. 224–42.

D41 "The Social Function of Open Spaces,"
in *Space for Living*. Edited by Sylvia Crowe. Amsterdam: Djambatan, 1961. pp. 22–40.

An address presented before the International Federation of Landscape Architects, 7th Annual Congress, held in Amsterdam, June 20–22, 1960.

Included in two of the collections of Mumford's essays: *The Highway and the City* (1963) and *The Urban Prospect* (1968) with the title "Landscape and Townscape."

D42 "Technology and Democracy,"
in *Challenges to Democracy: The Next Ten Years*. Edited by

Edward Reed. With an introduction by Robert M. Hutchins. New York: Frederick A. Praeger, 1963. pp. 33–44.

An address given at the Tenth Anniversary Convocation of the Fund for the Republic, New York City, January 21, 1963.

D43 "Utopia, the City and the Machine,"
in *Utopias and Utopian Thought*. Edited by Frank E. Manuel. Boston: Houghton Mifflin, 1966. pp. 3–24.

This essay first appeared in *Daedalus*, XCIV (Spring 1965), 271–92.

D44 "Closing Statement,"
in *Future Environments of North America*. Being the record of a conference convened by the Conservation Foundation in April 1965, at Airlie House, Warrenton, Virginia. Garden City, New York: Natural History Press, 1966. pp. 718–29.

D45 "In the Defense of the City,"
in *Metropolitan Politics*. Edited by Michael Danielson. Boston: Little, Brown and Co., 1966. pp. 20–27.

First published with the title "On Guard! The City Is in Danger!" in *University, A Princeton Quarterly*, no. 24 (Spring 1965), 10–13.

D46 "Technics and the Nature of Man,"
in *Knowledge among Men; Eleven Essays on Science, Culture, and Society Commemorating the 200th Anniversary of the Birth of James Smithson*. Edited by Paul H. Oehser. Introduction by S. Dillon Ripley. New York: Simon and Schuster, 1966. pp. 126–42.

This is the prologue, with slight additions, to Mumford's *The Myth of the Machine: I. Technics and Human Development* (1967).

D47 "Town,"
in *Chambers's Encyclopaedia*. New revised edition. Oxford: Pergamon Press Ltd., 1967. XIII, 718.

D48 "Historical Aspects" [of the Vietnam War,]
in *Authors Take Sides on Vietnam*. London: Peter Owen, 1967. pp. 179–80.

D49 "City: Forms and Functions,"
in *International Encyclopedia of the Social Sciences*. New York: Macmillan Co. and the Free Press, 1968. II, 447–55.

D50 "Patrick Geddes,"
in *International Encyclopedia of the Social Sciences*. New York: Macmillan Co. and the Free Press, 1968. VI, 81–83.

D51 "Machines,"
in *Encyclopedia Americana.* International edition. New York: Americana Corporation, 1968. XVIII, 57–62.

D52 "The Significance of Back Bay Boston,"
in *Back Bay Boston: The City as a Work of Art.* Boston: Museum of Fine Arts, 1969. pp. 18–20+.

D53 "Survival of Plants and Man,"
in *Challenge for Survival; Land, Air, and Water for Man in Megalopolis.* Edited by Pierre Dansereau. New York: Columbia University Press, 1970. pp. 221–35.

This essay, printed here with slight changes, was originally published in *Garden Journal*, XVIII (May/June 1968), 66–71.

ADDENDUM

D54 "The Value of Local History,"
in Dutchess County Historical Society (Poughkeepsie, N.Y.). *Yearbook, 1927.* pp. 22–26.

Paper read at Troutbeck (Amenia, N.Y.), September 15, 1926.

E. LETTERS TO THE EDITOR

NOTE: Mumford's letters written to periodicals responding to criticism of his articles in those periodicals are listed where the original articles are cited in this bibliography.

E1 "Constructive Criticism."
    Freeman, I (March 24, 1920), 34–35.

E2 "A Study in Social Distemper."
    Freeman, II (February 9, 1921), 519–20.

E3 "By Way of Explanation."
    Freeman, III (March 30, 1921), 66.

E4 [Comments on Robert Lynd's *The Passion of Labour*.]
    Freeman, III (June 1, 1921), 286.

E5 "The Pragmatic Acquiescence: A Reply."
    New Republic, XLIX (January 19, 1927), 250–51.

    Addressed to John Dewey.

E6 [A Communication.]
    Sociological Review, XXI (July 1929), 252–53.

E7 "Toward a Publication of [Charles S.] Peirce's Works."
    New Republic, LXV (December 30, 1930), 195.

E8 "The Uneconomic Mooring Mast" [on the Empire State Building.]
    New York Times, June 13, 1931, p. 14.

E9 "Parks and Bridges."
    New Republic, LXIX (December 30, 1931), 192.

E10 "Esthetics and Public Works."
    New Republic, LXXV (August 9, 1933), 344.

E11 "Roosevelt and Public Works."
    New Republic, LXXVI (October 11, 1933), 243–44.

E12 "On the Road to Collectivism."
    New Republic, LXXXI (February 6, 1935), 361–62.

E13   "A Memorial for Geddes."
New Republic, LXXXVI (March 4, 1936), 112.

The same letter, asking for funds to endow Outlook Tower and to support the editing of Patrick Geddes' papers, appeared with the title "Memorial to a Great Planner" in *American City*, LI (March 1936), 101.

E14   "Mr. Moses' Plan Criticized."
New York Times, December 3, 1938, p. 18.

Signed by Mumford and seven others. A second letter, replying to Mr. Moses' response to the letter of December 3, was published in the *New York Times*, December 14, 1938, p. 24. The same individuals signed the second letter.

E15   "Embargo Against Reich."
New York Times, Section IV (September 17, 1939), p. 9.

E16   "Resignations Accepted."
New Republic, CII (June 10, 1940), 795.

Mumford's letter of resignation as contributing editor expressing strong disapproval of the magazine's irresolute stand against fascism. Waldo Frank's letter of resignation also was published in this issue.

E17   "Food, for Revolt."
New York Herald Tribune, October 3, 1940, p. 22.

In reply to criticism of this letter, Mumford wrote another letter with the title "Norway's Brave Stand," which was published in the *New York Herald Tribune*, October 14, 1940, p. 16.

E18   "Two Letters from Readers."
New Republic, CV (September 8, 1941), 311–12.

Mumford's letter supports an editorial calling for the declaration of war against the Axis.

E19   [Letter to John Chamberlain, Book Editor.]
New York Times, August 29, 1942, p. 13.

This letter appeared in Mr. Chamberlain's column "Books of the Times." Mumford discusses American literary criticism of the 1920's.

E20   "Garden City v. Suburbanism."
New Republic, CX (January 10, 1944), 55.

Mumford comments further on this topic in the same volume, issue of February 28, 1944, p. 283.

E21 "Roman Account Stirs Reader; Protests Judgments of Mob Made by Mr. Matthews [*New York Times* correspondent] at Fascist's Trial."
New York Times, September 28, 1944, p. 18.

E22 "Mr. Beard and His 'Basic History.'"
Saturday Review of Literature, XXVII (December 2, 1944), 27.

E23 "Youth Conscription Called Callous."
New York Herald Tribune, December 14, 1944, p. 22.

E24 "Stop and Think."
Progressive Architecture-Pencil Points, XXVII (April 1946), 10.

Criticism of Kenneth Reid's proposal for a United Nations building.

E25 "A Letter from Lewis Mumford, Hon. M.T.P.I."
Town Planning Institute. Journal, XXXII (September-October 1946), 229.

Expresses gratitude to the Town Planning Institute for conferring honorary membership on him.

E26 "City Hall and Queens College."
New York Herald Tribune, February 23, 1949, p. 22.

E27 "Encyclopedic Errors."
Saturday Review of Literature, XXXII (June 25, 1949), 28.

E28 "Moral Implications of Our Atomic War Policy."
New York Herald Tribune, Section 2 (July 3, 1949), p. 5.

E29 "Our Military Policy. Reliance on Atom Warfare Said to Defeat Our Goals."
New York Times, Section IV (June 11, 1950), p. 8.

E30 "America's Unpreparedness."
New York Herald Tribune, August 7, 1950, p. 10.

E31 "Against Draft of 18-Year-Olds."
New York Times, January 20, 1951, p. 14.

E32 "'The Black Silence of Fear.'"
New York Times Magazine, January 27, 1952, p. 5.

Mumford's comments on Associate Supreme Court Justice William

O. Douglas's article in the *Times* with the above title. Suggests Douglas as Democratic presidential candidate.

E33 "Policy on [Hydrogen] Bomb Examined."
New York Times, Section IV (March 28, 1954), p. 10.

Included in the collection of Mumford's essays and other writings, *The Human Prospect* (1955), as a "Postscript" to the essay entitled "Program for Survival." Also included in William A. Williams, ed. *The Shaping of American Diplomacy*. Chicago: Rand McNally and Co., 1956. pp. 1028–30.

Mumford says this met the widest response of all his letters to the editor. He received over 100 responses, nearly all commendatory.

E34 "War Weapons Condemned."
New York Times, Section IV (November 27, 1955), p. 8.

E35 "A Communication."
Washington Post, November 11, 1957, p. A-15.

Mumford comments on Soviet launching of two satellites.

E36 "To Change China Policy."
New York Times, Section IV (September 28, 1958), p. 8.

E37 "Making Nuclear Decisions; Right of Specialists to Determine Fate of Populations Challenged."
New York Times, July 6, 1959, p. 26.

E38 "10th Anniversary Letters."
Landscape, X (Fall 1960), 5.

Mumford's tribute to *Landscape* on its tenth anniversary.

E39 " 'Strangelove' Reactions."
New York Times, Section II (March 1, 1964), p. 8.

Mumford comments on the theme of the motion picture "Dr. Strangelove."

E40 "F. D. R. [Franklin D. Roosevelt] Memorial."
New York Times, Section IV (August 16, 1964), p. 8.

E41 "Lettre de M. Lewis Mumford."
Comprendre (Société Européene de Culture), no. 28 (1965), 273.

Explains his opposition to U.S. Vietnam policy and his fears of its consequences.

E42 "Playing Russian Roulette in Vietnam."
San Francisco Chronicle, March 3, 1965, p. 38.

Also published in the *St. Louis Post-Dispatch*, March 3, 1965, p. 2-B, with the title "A Letter to the President."

E43 "Michael Gold."
Catholic Worker, XXXIII (July/August 1967), 8.

Mumford's comments on the occasion of the death of the contemporary author.

E44 "The Pentagon of Power."
New York Times Book Review, January 10, 1971, p. 36+.

Mumford's reply to criticism of *The Myth of the Machine: II. The Pentagon of Power* (1970) published in the review by Professor Gerald Holton in the *New York Times Book Review*, December 13, 1970.

F. PREFACES, FOREWORDS, INTRO-
DUCTIONS, AND EPILOGUES

F1 *American Architecture of the Twentieth Century; A Series of Photographs and Measured Drawings of Modern, Civic, Commercial and Industrial Buildings.*
Edited by Oliver Reagan.
With a preface by Lewis Mumford. New York: Architectural Book Publishing Co., 1927. 2 vols.

F2 *The Interpreter Geddes, the Man and His Gospel.*
by Amelia D. Defries.
With a foreword by Rabindranath Tagore and an introduction by Israel Zangwill; preface by Lewis Mumford. New York: Boni and Liveright, 1927.

Same preface also included in British edition: London: G. Routledge and Sons, 1927.

This preface is a reprint of Mumford's article, "Who *Is* Patrick Geddes?", published in *Survey Graphic*, LIII (February 1, 1925), 523–24.

F3 *Erewhon and Erewhon Revisited.*
by Samuel Butler.
Introduction by Lewis Mumford. New York: Modern Library, 1927.

F4 *Thomas H. Benton.*
With an introduction by Lewis Mumford. New York: New Gallery, [1927?].

A four-page catalog for the Benton exhibit.

F5 *A Scholar's Testament. Two Letters from George Edward Woodberry to J. E. Spingarn.*
With an introductory note by Lewis Mumford. Amenia, New York: Privately printed at the Troutbeck Press, 1931.

F6 *Planned Society: Yesterday, Today, Tomorrow; A Symposium by Thirty-Five Economists, Sociologists, and Statesmen.*

Edited by Findlay Mackenzie.
With a foreword by Lewis Mumford. New York: Prentice-Hall, Inc., 1937.

F7 *Roofs for 40 Millions, An Exhibition on Housing.*
by American Group, Inc.
With a foreword by Lewis Mumford. New York: Sheridan Square Press, [1938].

F8 *Robert Gair; A Study.*
by H. Allen Smith.
With an introduction by Lewis Mumford. New York: Dial Press, 1939.

F9 *Greenbelt.*
by O. Kline Fulmer.
With an introduction by Lewis Mumford. Washington, D.C.: American Council on Public Affairs, 1941.

F10 "Politics and the Poet."
by J. E. Spingarn.
Introduction by Lewis Mumford. *Atlantic Monthly*, CLXX (November 1942), 73–78.

F11 *Patrick Geddes, Maker of the Future.*
by Philip Boardman.
With an introduction by Lewis Mumford. Chapel Hill: University of North Carolina, 1944.

F12 *Warsaw Lives Again.*
by Stanislaw Albrecht.
Introduction by Lewis Mumford. Published by Committee on Exhibition, "Warsaw Lives Again," 1946.

F13 *Garden Cities of Tomorrow.*
by Ebenezer Howard.
Edited, with a preface by F. J. Osborn. With an introductory essay by Lewis Mumford. London: Faber and Faber, 1946.

Reprinted in 1965 and issued as a Faber Paper Covered Edition.

Reprinted and published in the United States as follows:

Cambridge, Mass.: M.I.T. Paperback Series, M.I.T. Press, 1965.

F14 *Patrick Geddes in India.*
Edited by Jacqueline Tyrwhitt.
With an introduction by Lewis Mumford, and a preface by H. V. Lancaster. London: L. Humphries, 1947.

F15   *The Family Log; Families, like Ships, Keep Records.*
Edited by Kenneth S. Beam.
With a foreword by Lewis Mumford. San Diego, California:
Special Projects Continuation Committee, [1947].

F16   *Conurbation, A Planning Survey of Birmingham and the Black
Country.*
by the West Midland Group.
With a foreword by Lewis Mumford. London: Architectural Press,
1948.

F17   *A Full Life in the Country; The Sudbury and District Plan.*
by Keith Jeremiah.
With a foreword by Lewis Mumford. London: B. T. Batsford, Ltd.,
1949.

F18   *Toward New Towns for America.*
by Clarence S. Stein.
With an introduction by Lewis Mumford. Liverpool: University
Press of Liverpool; agents for the Western Hemisphere: Public Administration Service, Chicago, 1951.

Revised edition, retaining Mumford's introduction of the earlier edition, published as follows:

New York: Reinhold Publishing Co., 1957.

Reprint of the 1957 edition published as follows:

Cambridge, Mass.: M.I.T. Press, 1966.

F19   *Our World from the Air; An International Survey of Man and His
Environment.*
by Erwin A. Gutkind.
With a foreword by G. P. Gooch and an introduction by Lewis
Mumford. Garden City, N.Y.: Doubleday and Co., 1952.

F20   *Europe, A Journey with Pictures.*
by Anne Fremantle and Bryan Holme.
Foreword by Lewis Mumford. New York: Studio Publications in
association with Thomas Y. Crowell, 1954.

F21   *Pennsylvania Triangle*, XLII (January 1956), 11.
Mumford wrote an introduction for this issue of the publication of
the students of the Fine Arts and Engineering Schools of the University of Pennsylvania.

F22   *Form in Civilization; Collected Papers on Art and Labour.* 2d edition.
by William R. Lethaby.

With a foreword by Lewis Mumford. London: Oxford University Press, 1957.

F23 *Walls: Res Sanctae/Res Sacrae.*
A passage from *Versuch ueber die Graebersymbolik der Alten.* Translated by B. Q. Morgan and with a note on J. J. Bachofen by Lewis Mumford. Lexington, Ky.: Stamperia del Santuccio, 1961.

F24 *Notre Dame of Paris.*
by Allan Temko.
With an introduction by Lewis Mumford. New York: Time Incorporated, 1962.

F25 *The New Exploration; A Philosophy of Regional Planning.*
by Benton MacKaye.
With an introduction by Lewis Mumford. Urbana: University of Illinois Press, 1962.

F26 *Mont-Saint-Michel and Chartres.*
by Henry Adams.
With an introduction by Lewis Mumford. New York: Collier Books, 1963.

F27 *The New Towns; The Answer to Megalopolis.*
by Frederick J. Osborn and Arnold Whittick.
With an introduction by Lewis Mumford. New York: McGraw-Hill, 1963.

Same edition published in Great Britain as follows:

London: Leonard Hill, 1963.

F28 *Portmeirion, the Place and Its Meaning.*
by Clough Williams-Ellis.
With photographs by Edwin Smith and an epilogue by Lewis Mumford. London: Faber and Faber, 1963.

Mumford's epilogue is an extract from his article "From Crotchet Castle to Arthur's Seat," *New Yorker,* XXXVII (January 13, 1962), 82+.

F29 *Rebuilding Cities.*
by Percy Johnson-Marshall.
With an introduction by Lewis Mumford. Chicago: Aldine Publishing Co., 1966.

F30 *Design with Nature.*
by Ian L. McHarg.

With an introduction by Lewis Mumford. Garden City, N.Y.: published for the American Museum of Natural History by the Natural History Press, 1969.

F31   *The Van Wyck Brooks–Lewis Mumford Letters: The Record of a Literary Friendship, 1921–1963.*
Edited by Robert E. Spiller.
With an introduction ("The Beginnings of a Friendship") by Lewis Mumford. E. P. Dutton and Co., 1970.

G. WORKS EDITED OR CO-EDITED

G1 "Regional Plan Number."
Survey Graphic, LIV (May 1, 1925), 128–206.

Mumford "collaborated with the editors in preparing the issue as a whole." Editor's note.

G2 *The American Caravan; A Yearbook of American Literature.*
New York: The Macaulay Co., 1927–31.
Editors: 1927, Van Wyck Brooks, Alfred Kreymborg, Lewis Mumford, and Paul Rosenfeld; 1928–1936, Alfred Kreymborg, Lewis Mumford, and Paul Rosenfeld.

Title varies: 1927, *The American Caravan: A Yearbook of American Literature*. Also published in the same year with the imprint of The Literary Guild of America, New York.
1928, *The Second American Caravan; A Yearbook of American Literature*.
1929, *The New American Caravan; A Yearbook of American Literature*.
1931, *American Caravan IV*.
1936, *The New Caravan*. New York: W. W. Norton & Co., 1936.

G3 *America and Alfred Stieglitz; A Collective Portrait.*
Edited by Waldo Frank, Lewis Mumford, Dorothy Norman, Paul Rosenfeld, and Harold Rugg. Garden City, N.Y.: Doubleday, Doran and Co., 1934. 339p.

Also published in 1934 as a Literary Guild of America (New York) edition.

G4 *Roots of Contemporary American Architecture; A Series of Thirty-Seven Essays Dating from the Mid-Nineteenth Century to the Present.*
Edited by Lewis Mumford.
New York: Reinhold Publishing Co., 1952. 454p.

The first section of the book, pages 3–30, contains an essay by Mumford with the title "A Backward Glance."

Reprinted with the same title and with a new preface by Mumford as follows:

New York: Grove Press, 1959. 454p.

Also published by Grove Press in the same year in a paperback (Evergreen) edition.

G5 *Essays and Journals.*
by Ralph Waldo Emerson.
Selected, and with an introduction by Lewis Mumford. Garden City, N.Y.: Doubleday & Co., 1968. 671p.

H. OTHER WORKS

WORKS WRITTEN IN COLLABORATION WITH OTHERS

H1 "Regional Planning."
Encyclopaedia Britannica. 14th edition. London: Encyclopaedia Britannica Co., Ltd., 1929. XIX, 71–72.

Benton MacKaye is co-author of this article.

H2 "Townless Highways for the Motorist."
Harper's Magazine, CLXIII (August 1931), 347–56.

Benton MacKaye is co-author of this essay.

H3 "Planned Community."
Architectural Forum, LVIII (April 1933), 253–54.

Article signed by Mumford and six others as members of the Committee on Housing Exhibition, Clarence S. Stein, chairman.

H4 *The Fair of the Future, 1939; Social Theme, Physical Concept, Design Organization, Summary.*
Submitted by the Committee formed at the dinner at the City Club, Wednesday, December 11, 1935. Michael Meredith Hare, Secretary. [New York]: Office of the Secretary, [1936]. 23p. (Mimeographed.)

Mumford was a member of the Committee submitting the report.

CONGRESSIONAL TESTIMONY

H5 U.S. Congress. Senate. Committee on Government Operations. *Federal Role in Urban Affairs. Hearings* before a Subcommittee on Executive Reorganization, 90th Cong., 1st sess., April 20–21, 1967, part 17, pp. 3595–3625.

Mumford's formal statement, but not the question and answer period that followed, included in the collection of Mumford's essays, *The Urban Prospect* (1968), with the title "A Brief History of Urban Frustration."

FILM COMMENTARY

H6   *The City.*
Produced by American Institute of Planners with a grant from the Carnegie Corporation, 1939.
Major part of commentary written by Lewis Mumford; narrated by Morris Carnovsky.
Musical score by Aaron Copeland.
Photographed and directed by Ralph Steiner and Willard Van Dyke.
31 minutes, black and white.

Excerpts from Mumford's commentary published in *Architectural Review,* LXXXVI (August 1939), 93–94.

H7   *Lewis Mumford on the City.*
Based on Mumford's book, *The City in History* (1961).
Produced and written by Ian MacNeill for the National Film Board of Canada, 1963.
Released in the United States by Sterling Educational Films, 1964.
Narrated in part by Lewis Mumford.
In six parts, each 28 minutes, black and white:

Part 1. The City: Heaven and Hell.

Part 2. The City: Cars or People?

Part 3. The City and Its Region.

Part 4. The Heart of the City.

Part 5. The City as Man's Home.

Part 6. The City and the Future.

CARTOONS

H8   "Modern Interior."
Survey, LV (November 15, 1925), 192.

H9   "Skyscrapers of the Future."
Survey, LV (December 15, 1925), 336.

I. BRITISH EDITIONS OF BOOKS

I1   *The Story of Utopias.*
       With an introduction by Hendrik Willem Van Loon. London:
       G. G. Harrap and Co., 1923. 315p.

I2   *The Golden Day; A Study in American Experience and Culture.*
       London: Humphrey Milford, 1927. 283p.

I3   *Herman Melville.*
       London: Jonathon Cape, 1929. 377p.

       Revised edition published with the title *Herman Melville, A Study
       of His Life and Vision.* London: Martin Secker and Warburg, 1963.
       256p.

I4   *Technics and Civilization.*
       London: G. Routledge and Sons, 1934. 495p.

       Reprinted with the same title and published as follows:

       London: Routledge and Kegan Paul, 1955. 495p.

       London: Routledge and Kegan Paul, 1962. 495p.

I5   *The Culture of Cities.*
       London: Martin Secker and Warburg, 1938. 586p.

I6   *Men Must Act.*
       London: Martin Secker and Warburg, 1939. 222p.

I7   *Faith for Living.*
       London: Martin Secker and Warburg, 1941. 247p.

       Contains a special preface not in the American edition.

I8   *The Condition of Man.*
       London: Martin Secker and Warburg, 1944. 467p.

       Reprinted with the same title and published as follows:

       London: Mercury Books, 1963. 467p.

I9   *City Development; Studies in Disintegration and Renewal.*
       London: Martin Secker and Warburg, 1946. 199p.

I10 *Programme for Survival.*
London: Martin Secker and Warburg, 1946. 67p.

A chapter with this title taken from Mumford's book, *Values for Survival* (1946).

I11 *The Conduct of Life.*
London: Martin Secker and Warburg, 1952. 342p.

I12 *Art and Technics.*
London: Oxford University Press, 1952. 162p.

I13 *The Human Prospect.*
Edited by Harry T. Moore and Karl W. Deutsch. London: Martin Secker and Warburg, 1956. 319p.

I14 *The Transformations of Man.*
World Perspectives, Vol. 6. London: George Allen & Unwin, 1957. 192p.

This edition contains additional material in Chapters 6 and 8, not included in the American (Harper and Brothers) edition.

I15 *The City in History: Its Origins, Its Transformations, and Its Prospects.*
London: Martin Secker and Warburg, 1961. 657p.

Reprinted with the same title and published as follows:

[Harmondsworth]: Penguin Books, 1966. 695p.

I16 *The Highway and the City.*
London: Martin Secker and Warburg, 1964. 189p.

Includes a special preface by Mumford for this edition.

I17 *The Myth of the Machine: I. Technics and Human Development.*
London: Martin Secker and Warburg, 1967. 342p.

This is the first volume of a two-volume work; the second volume scheduled for publication in 1971.

I18 *The Urban Prospect.*
London: Martin Secker and Warburg, 1968. 255p.

I19 *The Myth of the Machine: II. The Pentagon of Power.*
London: Martin Secker and Warburg. To be published in 1971.

This is the second volume of a two-volume work; the first volume published in 1967.

J. FOREIGN-LANGUAGE EDITIONS OF BOOKS

Note: Titles are listed in order of their original publication in the United States. This list is intended primarily to demonstrate the universal interest that has been shown in Mumford's work. It is not meant to be a comprehensive bibliography of his foreign-language editions.

J1   *The Story of Utopias.*

Italian: Calderini, 1969.

J2   *Sticks and Stones.*

German: Bruno Cassirer Verlag, 1925.
Russian: Publisher (?), 1936.

J3   *Herman Melville.*

Italian: Edizioni di Comunita, 1965.

J4   *The Brown Decades.*

Spanish: Ediciones Infinito, 1960.

J5   *Technics and Civilization.*

Czech: Prace, [1947].
French: Editions du Seuil, 1950.
Italian: Il Saggiatore, 1961.
Japanese: Kamakura Shobo, 1954.
Polish: Panstwowe Wydawnictwo Naukowe, 1966.
Swedish: Kooperativa Forbundet Bokforlaget, [1949].
Vietnamese: USIA (Department of National Education), n.d.

J6   *The Culture of Cities.*

Finnish: Werner Soderstrom Osakeyhtio, 1949.
Italian: Edizioni di Comunita, 1953.
Japanese: Maruzen, 1955.
Portuguese: Editora Itatiaia, 1961.
Spanish: Emecé Editores, 1946.
Swedish: Kooperativa Forbundet, n.d.

J7   *The Social Foundations of Post-War Building.*

Danish: Nordisk, n.d.
Dutch: H. P. Leopold, 1946.

J8   *The Condition of Man.*

German: Infantry Journal, n.d.
Italian: Edizioni di Comunita, 1965.
Italian: Etas Kompass, 1967.
Japanese: Infantry Journal, 1950.
Korean: Infantry Journal, 1950.
Portuguese: Livaria do Globo, 1953.
Spanish: Compania General Fabril Editora, 1961.
Swedish: Kooperativa Forbundet Bokforlaget, n.d.

J9   *City Development; Studies in Disintegration and Renewal.*

Danish: Nordisk Forlag Arnold Busk, n.d.
German: Infantry Journal, 1951.

J10   *The Conduct of Life.*

Japanese: Riososha Press, 1956.
Portuguese: Editora Itatiaia, 1959.

J11   *Art and Technics.*

German: W. Kohlhammer, 1959.
Spanish: Nueva Visión, n.d.

J12   *In the Name of Sanity.*

Italian: Edizioni di Comunita, 1959.
Italian: Etas Kompass, 1968.
Swedish: Kooperativa Forbundet Bokforlaget, 1956.

J13   *From the Ground Up.*

French: USIA (Seghers), 1965.
Portuguese: USIA (Fondo de Cultura), 1965.

J14   *The Transformations of Man.*

German: Ullstein Verlag, 1961.
Italian: Edizioni di Comunita, 1968.
Japanese: Bijutsu Shuppan-sha, 1958.
Spanish: Editorial Sur, 1961.

J15   *The City in History: Its Origins, Its Transformations, and Its Prospects.*

Arabic: Franklin Publications, 1964.
French: Editions du Seuil, 1964.
German: Kiepenheuer & Witsch, 1963.
Hindi: Government of India, n.d.
Italian: Etas Kompass, 1967.
Japanese: Shincho Sha, 1968.
Serbo-Croat: Naprijed, 1968.
Spanish: Ediciones Infinito, 1965.

J16　*The Highway and the City.*

Spanish: Emecé Editores, 1966.

J17　*The Myth of the Machine: I. Technics and Human Development.*

Italian: Il Saggiatore, 1970.

J18　*The Urban Prospect.*

Spanish: Emecé, 1970.

APPENDIX: MANUSCRIPT MATERIAL

THIS brief section is intended to assist anyone wishing to locate manuscript collections of Lewis Mumford's writings and correspondence. It is just a starting point as the list is limited to collections cited in two sources: *National Union Catalog of Manuscript Collections.* Compiled by the Library of Congress. Washington: Library of Congress, 1962–. *American Literary Manuscripts; A Checklist of Holdings in Academic, Historical and Public Libraries in the United States.* Compiled by the Modern Language Association: American Literature Group, Committee on Manuscript Holdings. Austin, Texas: University of Texas, 1960. As each list has used a different method to describe the collections it includes, I have separated the listings accordingly. The bulk of Mumford's original manuscripts is still (1970) in his home in Amenia, New York.

NATIONAL UNION CATALOG

Manuscript collections of Mumford's papers:

American Academy of Arts and Letters Library, New York City.
Mumford correspondence, 1930–
About 100 items relating to the National Institute of Arts and Letters, and the American Academy of Arts and Letters.
Open to investigators under restrictions accepted by the library.

Manuscript collections containing correspondence of Mumford:

George Biddle.
Papers, 1899–1960.
In Library of Congress, Manuscript Division, Washington, D.C.
Part of the collection is closed to investigators.

Westgate Press, San Francisco, California.
Correspondence, 1929–1931.
Relates primarily to the choice of material for publication.

Albert L. Guérard.
Correspondence, 1909–1959.
In Stanford University Libraries, Stanford, California.
Unpublished register in the library.

Emil Lorch.
> Papers, 1891–1963.
> In University of Michigan, Michigan Historical Collections, Ann Arbor, Michigan.

John T. Flynn.
> Papers, 1928–1961.
> In University of Oregon Library, Eugene, Oregon.
> Inventory published by the University of Oregon Library.
> Open to investigators under restrictions accepted by the library.

Isidore Schneider.
> Papers, 1925–1965.
> In Columbia University Libraries, New York City.

Van Wyck Brooks.
> Papers, 1898–1963.
> In University of Pennsylvania Libraries, Philadelphia, Pennsylvania.
> Case file in the library.
> Open to investigators under library restrictions.

Waldo Frank.
> Papers, 1900–1960.
> In University of Pennsylvania Libraries, Philadelphia, Pennsylvania.
> Descriptive case file available in library.

AMERICAN LITERARY MANUSCRIPTS; A CHECKLIST OF HOLDINGS IN ACADEMIC, HISTORICAL AND PUBLIC LIBRARIES IN THE UNITED STATES

Although this volume lists very small collections, I have omitted those collections with fewer than ten letters.

Yale University, New Haven, Connecticut.
> 74 letters.

New York Public Library, New York City.
> Significant holdings; no count given or type of material described.

Viking Press, New York City.
> Publisher's collection. Significant holdings of letters, but no count given.

Dartmouth College, Hanover, New Hampshire.
> Four manuscripts.

Princeton University, Princeton, New Jersey.
  Significant holdings. Type of material and number of items not given.

Cleveland Public Library, Cleveland, Ohio.
  One manuscript.

State Historical Society, Madison, Wisconsin.
  Significant holdings of letters, but no count given.

ADDENDUM: The collection of letters referred to by Mr. Mumford in the introduction to this bibliography deserves a separate listing here:

National Library of Scotland, Edinburgh.
  Letters of Lewis Mumford to Patrick Geddes and Victor Branford, 1920–1932.

INDEX

INDEX

NOTE: Titles of books and pamphlets written by Lewis Mumford are shown in capital letters. Other book and pamphlet titles, and all periodical titles, are italicized. Titles of articles, short stories, poems, and letters to the editor appear in quotation marks. Citations are referred to by item number.